MATÍAS PREISWERK is the *Educación cristiana (1982) and* Los seño-res del gran poder *(1986).*

EDUCATING
IN THE LIVING WORD

Matías Preiswerk

EDUCATING
IN THE LIVING WORD

A THEORETICAL FRAMEWORK
FOR CHRISTIAN EDUCATION

Translated from the Spanish
by Robert R. Barr

ORBIS BOOKS

Maryknoll, New York 10545

The Catholic Foreign Mission Society of America (Maryknoll) recruits and trains
people for overseas missionary service. Through Orbis Books Maryknoll aims to
foster the international dialogue that is essential to mission. The books published,
however, reflect the opinions of their authors and are not meant to represent the
official position of the society.

First published as *Educar en la palabra viva: marco teórico para la educación
cristiana*, © 1984 by Comisión Evangélica Latinoamericana de Educación Cristiana
(CELADEC), Lima, Peru

English translation © 1987 by Orbis Books, Maryknoll, NY 10545
Manufactured in the United States of America

Manuscript editor: Lisa McGaw

Library of Congress Cataloging-in-Publication Data
Preiswerk, Matías.
  Educating in the living word.

  Translation of: Educar en la palabra viva.
  Bibliography: p.
  1. Christian education—Philosophy.   2. Christian
education—Latin America.   3. Liberation theology.
4. Catholic Church—Education—Latin America.
BV1464.P7313   1987   207'.8   87-9221
ISBN 0-88344-572-7
ISBN 0-88344-571-9 (pbk.)

Contents

v

Foreword

As part of our continuing effort in support of the churches, and of the many groups of Christian educators, we wish to share this study guide: *Educating in the Living Word: A Theoretical Framework for Christian Education.* Many Christian educators in Latin America are constantly engaged in self-questioning as to their role in the liberation processes of the continent, especially in their specific capacity as agents of a Christian approach to the work of education. This study guide seeks to come to their assistance with a frame of reference for Christian education, and as a point of departure for a dialogue among those who feel the need of ongoing support in their Christian practice as educators. This support is precisely the objective of these pages. We hope we may help make Christian educational practice become ever more consistent, and ever more historically committed to the dispossessed.

CELADEC
(Latin American Evangelical Commission
for Christian Education)

Preface

The title of this book is admittedly pretentious. The discovery of a theoretical framework for Christian education in our times, amid the conflicts of a continent hovering between life and death, will be no simple task.

Christian education, however, must be able to defend its existence—must "give an account of its hope"—in a situation in which, while few deny its usefulness, many devote themselves to its utilization for ends that are neither educational nor certainly Christian.

As we shall see, the quest for a theoretical framework for Christian education will not consist in grand academic disquisitions but, rather, in an interpretation and evaluation of the practice of an exploited and believing people who, while rejecting a society claiming to offer "education" and "Christian education," continue to educate themselves precisely in that transforming action in which their practice consists. The quest will be a complex undertaking, however, since it will involve abandonment of the narrow, pseudo-specialized viewpoint of the dominator, and the replacement of this viewpoint with the globalizing perspective of the people—an approach that will dismantle approaches to reality that have heretofore succeeded in representing themselves as "solid" and "scientific."

This book will take up various approaches to educational reality, and systematize them anew, from a point of departure of the "irruption of the poor" into all spheres of society, including the knowledge process. To be sure, we shall leave many routes without many signposts, in the hope that others will be able to map the way in greater detail from their own personal, practical experiences. The dynamics of our reflection will take its point of departure in the interpretation of a reality, and move from there to an attempt to formulate a framework that will issue in the transformation of that same reality.

In Part 1 we shall begin with the various practices of Christian education prevailing in Latin America, and arrive at three "moments" discernible in this phenomenon. In Part 2, in an attempt to read the Bible in the light of a critical view of reality, we shall perceive, within a great diversity of educational practices, one clearly liberative, popular approach. Part 3 will take the biblical perspective of the people, along with their practice, and indicate the principal routes of a relationship between a liberative Christian education and the global reality in which this education is called for.

Accordingly, this book will not be a manual for planning Christian education or a dissertation on its philosophy, objectives, methodology, and content. Our concern here is with one basic question: What does it mean to educate in Christian fashion—that is, to educate in and for life—in a society that uses its idols to educate for death?

PART 1

THE REALITY OF CHRISTIAN
EDUCATION AND ITS ANALYSIS

Given the objectives of this work, we cannot pretend to set forth a typology of all the models of Christian education competing in Latin America today. Still, in our quest for a Christian education that will respond to the challenges of the present hour, we must examine certain characteristic practices of this phenomenon called Christian education.

A practice of Christian education does not consist simply in a way of teaching, nor in a set of certain elements of content, nor in education's ties with certain institutions such as the local church, or a high school, or a base church community. Underlying Christian education we find a series of basic principles, explicit or implicit, conscious or unconscious, determining the shape of this education. In particular, we always find some specific type of commitment to the human being and to society.

In this first part of this work, we shall present three actual, historical examples of approaches to Christian education. Two of them are found in certain Christian-education materials. The third is the account of a real-life experience.

We shall endeavor to "read" these three practices, with the help of certain tools furnished by the social sciences, and to construct three specific models of Christian education—not from our own preconceptions, but from a critical analysis of actual reality.

1

1

Christian Education in Latin America:
Various Practices

Throughout the length and breadth of the Latin American continent, in many local churches, Catholic as well as Protestant, the term "Christian education" is used to refer to very different, and sometimes contrary and antagonistic, practices. Even one and the same church in one and the same place may abound with examples that illustrate this fact.

What we propose to do now is to set forth and analyze three examples of this diversity, in three different situations, moments, and churches, along with some little indication of their contextual situations.

CHRISTIAN EDUCATION IN THE SUNDAY SCHOOL

Among Protestants the primary instrument of Christian education is the "Sunday school." The name no longer corresponds very well to the reality, since the latter has undergone considerable deformation and reduction over the course of the centuries. The term was coined in the midst of the industrial revolution in England: certain Protestant churches offered miners' children, or the children of other poor laborers who had no opportunity to go to school during the week owing to inhuman working hours, the opportunity of some formal schooling on Sundays. This formation was integral, and included education in all primary subjects. The

3

faith element was contained in the global inspiration of the project, and was occasionally manifested in moments of celebration.

Over the years, however, the Sunday school movement came under the control of the dominant classes, and its content was reduced to the religious sphere, preferably in the areas of the Bible and morality. The missioners who brought Protestantism to Latin America were rarely capable of interpreting the local educational problematic, and promoted a "Sunday school" on what had become the traditional model—limited to religion and leaving the rest to the public school. In this conception, Christian education had a precise, limited framework and, furthermore, represented an institution in the strict sense, with relatively well-defined agencies, materials, and objectives.

The first example is taken from a Sunday school manual no longer used in Latin America, but which has been part of the upbringing of a number of generations of Protestants on the continent. It is now only a matter of record, happily one of the past. But it seems to us that the bygone use of this particular material is tremendously revealing for a conception of Christian education perhaps still too much present today.

We find, in the Pupil's Manual (for intermediate primary grades) of the *Curso Hispanoamericano de Educación Cristiana* ("Spanish-American Course in Christian Education") published in 1949, the following material:

LESSON SEVEN: A NEW IDEA OF THE KINGDOM

Bible references: Mark 4:3–33; 10:17–31; Luke 13:18–22

Chamba was an Indian boy, dirty, ignorant, and superstitious—but the son of a chief, and so he enjoyed greater privileges than did his playmates. His father had hopes that Chamba would succeed him as chief of the tribe, and so, with his future in mind, sent him to a mission school that had recently been established in a nearby village. There the boy found a strange world. He was given different clothes to wear. Most of his companions were civilized boys. His teachers were intelligent and friendly. It was a completely new life for him. Chamba made the most of his opportunities. Finishing his primary and secondary schooling, he entered the university, where he distinguished himself as an intelligent, well-trained young man. Then he thought of his father, his tribe, their customs, their ignorance, their misery. Chamba had begun to live and think as a modern man, and he wondered: "Can I be satisfied with jungle life? Can I return to my people and be happy?"

He received a business offer, and was tempted to stay in the modern world. A constant struggle raged within him. He felt the duty, the obligation to return and help his father and grandfather. And one day there he was, back among the tribal huts. Now the Indians regarded him with mistrust, envy, even a certain hostility, as if he were a foreigner, a stranger. And Chamba was disgusted by the savage practices, the filth, the ignorance, and the superstition that had not changed one whit since his childhood. He wanted to flee, to return to civilization and a comfortable life.

But something made Chamba stay. His father, who was old now, needed his support, and the people needed education. So Chamba founded a school, where he began to teach everyone, children and grownups, some of the precious knowledge that he had acquired. He had to combat superstitious ideas, ignorance, jealousy, envy, hatred, and opposition. But he persisted in his objective.

Savage customs and traditions are strong, and it was very difficult to dislodge them from the mind of Chamba's people. But little by little he introduced them to new ideas. He taught them to build better houses, to raise new crops and, most of all, to know Christ.

Chamba's experience is similar to that of Jesus among the Jews, attached as they were to their traditional ideals of religion and race. He taught them a completely new way. He taught as someone having more authority than the scribes and priests, and there were not a few to oppose these new ideas, so different from the ones to which they were accustomed.

This lesson deals with the way in which the priests and rabbis taught about the kingdom of God, and the way in which Jesus taught. It is difficult for us today to understand why Jesus' teachings caused such astonishment, for we are accustomed to them. . . .

This example may seem grotesque, or even foreign to the reality of certain parts of the continent. And yet, in some regions of Latin America, such as in the Andes, where the majority of the population is indigenous, a story like this causes no smiles. We know only too well what the result can be of this dichotomy between traditional Indian society (barbarism) and Western society (civilization). We are not yet far from the worldview of the Spanish Conquistadores of the sixteenth century, although we live in the twentieth century.

If we look for the qualifiers in the passage quoted above, and arrange these in two parallel columns, one for Chamba's people and the other for the new world he has discovered, we arrive at the following result, which needs no further commentary.

Indian World	*Civilized World*
Dirty (twice)	Missionary school
Ignorant (four times)	Different clothes
Superstitious (three times)	Civilized children
Misery	Intelligent, friendly people
Mistrust	New life
Envy (twice)	University
Hostility	Modern man
Savage practices	Comfortable life
Jealousy	Better houses
Hatred	New crops
Opposition	New ideas
Savage traditions	Knowing Christ

We are not interested in passing judgment on those who produced and distributed this kind of material in the past. We are interested in seeing how Christian education, despite its enclosure in an institution such as the Sunday school, whose content generally does not go beyond the biblical and the moral, can imply, in its examples, a wholly racist, dependent society.

The most curious thing about our example is without a doubt its biblical theology. What does Chamba's story have to do with the kingdom inaugurated by Jesus? We shall not find the answer in the biblical passages cited at the opening of the lesson, nor do we find it in the rest of the lesson, which we have not reprinted because Chamba is not mentioned again.

Will it be enough, then, to oppose the ideas, the customs, of one's milieu in order to be like Jesus in his practice of proclaiming the kingdom? Or could it be that the kingdom proclaimed by Jesus is precisely the civilization propagated by missioners in their "mission schools," like the one in our example? Such hypotheses will be suspect, at the very least.

CHRISTIAN EDUCATION IN SCHOOL RELIGION COURSES

The aftermath of Vatican Council II has seen a most significant renewal of Catholic religious education, both in the actual concept of religious education and in its methodology, hence of course in its materials. Without entering into detail, we may say that the main efforts of this renewal bear on a new anthropological foundation, with a point of departure in the contemporary human being and a presentation of the Christian message from this reality.

In Latin America the renewal in religious education has manifested itself particularly in the area of religion courses in the schools. The reason for this is that a very considerable number of the Latin American clergy are not involved in formal education. Thus impressive quantities of "religion books" have appeared everywhere, usually called *textos de catequesis escolar* ("school religion texts").

As in the previous example, the selection we are about to cite does not pretend to synthesize the wealth and complexity of this practice of Christian education. Neither do we seek to contrast it with the selection given above, which would be meaningless in view of the vast differences of context, aim, and method.

The example we reprint here is taken from a textbook intended for students of the second year of secondary school, entitled *Mi mundo de comunicación* ("My World of Communication"), published by Paulinas in 1981. The book has an attractive format, a modern design, stimulating photographs and drawings, and activities for the students.

COMMUNICATION WITH THE OTHER

Friendship and Communication

You are growing up. As you become more YOURSELF, you are coming to realize that you frequently encounter the "other." Who is the other? The other is whoever is around you—your classmates, boys and girls who go to the same school as you, who belong to the same club as you, or who are from the same neighborhood. There are many "others" around you.

And from among these "others," you choose your friends.

And from among your friends you choose your "best friend."

Friendship is something extraordinarily rich. I don't have to tell you that. You must already have experienced it.

You don't exactly know why you're somebody's friend. When you stop to think about it, you can't really find the reasons. "We just get along well, we're at ease with each other, we like each other, time flies when we're together, we understand each other, we help each other, we share things like our spare time, we study together, work together, we have the same problems, we like the same things, we unquestioningly trust each other."

But these aren't reasons. I remember something from Pascal that I copied into my notebook when I was in second year: "The heart has reasons that reason knows nothing of" (*Pensées,* IV, §277).

And that's true. That sentence sums up a very real idea. It's hard to explain, but that's the way it is!

Friendship is a deep Christian value.

Of course, you don't have to be a Christian to have friends. What I mean to say is that, if you have friends, whether you know it or not you are having a deep experience of love—and that is the essence of our religion, the essence of Jesus' message.

Friendship is self-surrender, sharing, coming out of oneself. It means you've beaten selfishness. It means you understand life as a community affair.

We say that friendship is a profound Christian value because we can discover Christ in friendship: true friends show us Jesus, through their actions, attitudes, and words.

And our encounter with the Lord multiplies and grows!

My Friend Jesus Christ

A great deal has been said about Jesus as a friend. He is *the* Friend. "There is no greater love than this: to lay down one's life for one's friends" (Jn. 15:13).

Christ gave his life for us—for us, his friends.

And I wonder—is this friendship a two-way street? Is Jesus our friend? How?

The Sacraments: Signs of a Friendship Encounter
with Jesus

Whenever two boys are friends, or two girls, or a boy and a girl, there are certain "signs" or signals—certain external things that you can see—that show to other people this friendship. We see these people together often, we see a special affection between them when they meet, or study together, or chat—or argue!

The SACRAMENTS are the external acts, the signs, that express our friendship with God. The sacraments are visible signs, instituted by Jesus, that reinforce and guarantee our relationship with him.

In the sacraments we have the fullest communication between the human being and GOD.

A SACRAMENT, then, is a sacred sign established by Christ to communicate his grace to us. Sacraments are VISIBLE actions, with words and gestures, in which Jesus, by his love and the power of the Holy Spirit, continues to be present among us.

They are the HIGH POINTS, the peak moments, in the life of a Christian and of the church, and so they come at the moment of important "passages," or steps, in people's lives.

The sacraments make it possible for us to express our love

for God. And JESUS expresses his presence among us. . . .

A shallow understanding of the sacraments means an empty spot in our relationship with God. To have received a sacrament, baptism for example, and to know just "a little bit" about it, is like shaking hands with a friend or kissing a friend out of habit, without content, without meaning.

A "phony smile" or a hug without any meaning doesn't express anything. It's a "black hole" in a starless night. It's a show of sincerity that will never satisfy anyone.

"THE SACRAMENTS ARE MOMENTS OF MEET-ING. IN THEM WE GROW, MATURE, AND MOVE CLOSER TO HAPPINESS."

The first thing that strikes us in this example is the style. The author tries to strike a direct relationship between the author (and through the author, the teacher) and the student, who is addressed directly.

But the style is a sign of something still more important. The author is taking the psychological and "affective" characteristics of the student seriously. The text appreciates the value of the human experience that the young person is undergoing, and starts with that, to arrive at elements of doctrine.

At the same time, it is to be observed that this eagerness for personalization or, better, individualization, completely ignores the world around, the world of conflict and inequality. Social conflicts are altogether absent. The world is reduced to the world of school and one's own social class. The world of the "other" is limited to "classmates, boys and girls who go to the same school as you, who belong to the same club as you, or who are from the same neighborhood." Friendship is described as a value lived within these social relationships—a value that does not cross its current boundaries.

With this situation as the point of departure, we now move to the doctrinal and theological plane, in a neatly inductive procedure. From the student's experience of friendship, he or she is asserted to be able to conclude to the manner and kind of friendship one may have with Jesus. The rather psychologizing outlook of the foregoing description will necessarily have repercussions here. A relationship with Jesus is not to be seen as essentially outside the series of relationships in the life of the young person and of his or her social class. A relationship of friendship with Jesus does not question the relationship of friendship with others (who, furthermore, are undifferentiated socially), but simply finds its model there.

Next, it would appear that a relationship of friendship with Jesus will be limited to, and exhausted in, the sacraments. Here we have a definite "leap" in the excellent anthropological perspective with which the lesson opens. And suddenly one's religious practice (exclusively?) guarantees one's relationship of friendship with Jesus and God, and one's friendship with others is reduced to a symbolic example.

It seems to us that we have a theological reductionism here, with deep repercussions in Latin America. If friendship with Jesus is to be found only in the faithful celebration of the sacraments, then one's religious life and practice can be lived out in a reality totally alien to the reality and conflicts of the life of the person's country and people. The radically "other," the oppressed, have nothing to do with a person's relationship of friendship with Jesus, and one's social practice of friendship has no reason to emerge from the ambient of one's friends and social class, nor any need to question the prevailing order of injustice—which is what actually prevents a person from being Jesus' friend.

Our somewhat polemical observations are not intended as a denial that the catechetical renewal has been positive for Christian education, particularly in the formation of the adolescent and an appreciation of the value of adolescent experiences. We wish only to call attention to the risk of emphasizing the existential and anthropological element exclusively, and of jumping from there to the doctrinal and theological without mentioning the social mediations so clearly present in the gospel message.

In sum, neither the anthropological accent nor the modernization of pedagogical materials and techniques can of themselves guarantee the fidelity of Christian education to the liberative gospel of Jesus Christ.

CHRISTIAN EDUCATION IN THE BASE COMMUNITIES

Christian education is conducted outside the churches and schools, as well as within them. New practices and manifestations are appearing, and are opening up new vistas.

An exploited, believing Latin American people, in many places and in various ways, is conducting a renewal of its own Christian education. The phenomenon is too rich and dynamic to be able to be pigeonholed in current pastoral or pedagogical categories. This is something that touches the life of the people in its global aspects and that, in order to be adequately understood and interpreted, requires a new "rationality." Thus Christian education as lived and practiced in the base church communities is overflowing its institutional banks and taking on new forms and new content. It is in the struggle against a death-dealing society that one learns the most, since it is from the heart of this struggle that Christ teaches.

The third example of an approach to Christian education, then, is taken from a pamphlet published in 1982 by the Campaña de Fraternidad in Brazil, in an area of São Paulo in which a variety of experiences, testimonials, and contributions could be gathered from different Christian communities. The pamphlet is entitled *CEBs: Universidad del Pueblo* ("The Base Communities: The People's University"). It has no intent of being a popular catechism or any sort of religious-education publication as such. We shall select a few passages from it, quoting some, summarizing others, in hopes of getting a view of the whole without taking up too much time and space in doing so.

THE BASE COMMUNITY AS THE PLACE WHERE POPULAR EDUCATION HAPPENS

The people are the agents of their own education.

There is a new presence in the base church community: the poor. Until now they have been here only as onlookers, passive in the presence of the word of God. Now they are agents of its interpretation. They integrate their faith and their life, God's word and reality. The power of the word of God, joined to the challenges of the everyday and the struggle for survival, have enabled the participants of the base communities to emerge from a fatalistic attitude, or one of a verbal practice—the manipulation of words—to arrive at an attitude of self-questioning, in which they can be the organizers of a new history. . . .

Hope

Some steps have already been taken. One of them is the Ministries School. . . . Here we see a service of concrete deeds rendered to one's sisters and brothers and the people of God. Two great motive forces stand behind this effort: a practice enlightened by the figure of the supreme Teacher, Jesus of Nazareth, and the challenge of reconstructing society so that all will be equal.

The first inspires an ongoing evaluation, a constant drawing up of accounts as to the progress of the group, in the critical mirror of Jesus' teaching, of his confrontation with the dominant power. In this way, theology is made a thing of the present, by practice lived in history. Faith leads us to a practice whose finality is none other than the building of a society of brothers and sisters. . . .

Street Groups

The "street groups" are bonds of union where the challenge is to practice democracy—groups of persons bound together by the hope and possibility of starting off down the road to what we might call the power of the brothers and sisters on the street. Street groups spring from the faith of the people. They are groups of persons who pray together and seek to bear witness to God's word through the healing of the sick, love for the marginalized and outcast, the struggle for truth, the sharing of bread, and so on. These persons do not act separately. The group itself decides what sort of group it will be, where and how it will help and share, and so on.

The appearance of group councils, or community councils—assemblies watching over unity of purpose and method, an equitable and viable distribution of tasks, and the socialization of power and knowledge, all accomplished through joint decision—is a sign that we are getting beyond a secular, bureaucratic, parochial scheme of things. These councils even question the consecrated forms of popular organization, as, for example, political power. Anything claiming for itself the absolute right to represent the people or a group of people will be hearing from these new forces and forms of representation.

Pilgrimages

It used to be the pastors who would organize pilgrimages. Today it is the poor. And no longer is it pilgrimage for the sake of pilgrimage: it is the march of Abraham, of Moses, of Jesus from Galilee to Jerusalem, and so on.

New Alternatives in Education

Until recently we thought that education took place in two special places: school and family. Parents and teachers were considered to be the ones responsible for the education of the community. . . . In the base communities, a new type of relationship among persons is making its appearance. Here, members' participation in the search for solutions to common problems, an exchange of experiences and opinions, and fellowship among members are occasioning changes in attitudes and ways of thinking among the persons who are part of these communities. This, too, is surely education. . . .

In this kind of education, the traditional division between educator and educated disappears. We are all educators and we are all being educated, because we are all being transformed and we are all engaged in the process of transforming others. In this pilgrimage of the people of God, we are indeed "verifying" a genuine experiment in fellowship, and experience of fellowship, in which no one simply educates anyone else, because no one is being educated alone. We are all educating one another. It is a new experiment and a new experience. We shall soon be able to evaluate its results in terms of the growth and maturation of the people of God.

Early Education in the Base Communities

Parents are gaining a new awareness. They now seek to obtain for their children a religious education that will defend them against an ongoing aggression on the part of society. . . .

Responding to the challenges of the peripheral urban slums, base communities do several things at once. They train religion teachers, they organize religious education, they sign up children as well as adults. These are not successive steps, they are parts of a single practice. . . . For example, in August and September of 1981, some two thousand children responded to a questionnaire on conditions in their families and neighborhoods, on parent-child relationships, and on the nutritional, educational, and recreational resources available to them.

On the [UN International] Day of the Child, the data thus obtained were used by the children and their mothers in a public denunciation of the deprivation in which slum children are forced to live. This joint protest was the collective action of children, religion teachers, mothers, and young people who had undergone three months' training. The religion teachers had devoted time and effort to the preparation of the questionnaire, the Day of the Child, and activities like dramatizations, posters, and so on.

Children who used to be rounded up for show or celebration are now being gradually mobilized in a planned, organized way. This does not mean that a sense of celebration is lost. It is maintained, but it is being gradually impregnated with a prophetic content of protest and hope.

Children are acquiring the habit of celebrating their faith, and being involved in joint training with their parents. And so their perception of their faith and a commitment to concrete struggle grow. . . .

Through these accounts of certain base community experiments, we catch a glimpse of the irruption of a new "subject," a new agent, into education in general and Christian education in particular: a poor people. The agent of education is no longer the pastoral minister (conservative or progressive), nor is the student any longer treated simply as an individual, in isolation from the conditions of his or her social class. The agent is now the people, who are eager to adopt the project of education as their own.

The people, organized in the base church communities, take on the task of their own education—not neglecting the contribution of those who have more training, but making their own decision as to the nature, content, and form of this education. The education in question has a number of particular characteristics. The first thing that strikes us is its breadth, together with its constant "reference" and orientation to the Bible—two intimately connected and reciprocally influential elements.

This capability of attacking any concrete problem, material or spiritual, in the community, is welded to a basis, a foundation, in the word of God. The importance of Bible study groups in the makeup of the base church communities in Brazil is significant: communities have been able to assimilate God's word and make it their own, and at the same time feel themselves to be interpreted by it. Thus the word of God accompanies the people in their struggle for a life of dignity, lends them strength to defeat a spirit of fatalism, nourishes their spiritual life, and corrects their political practice. In a word, it educates them. When God's word acquires a like globalism in the life of the people, Christian education cannot lag behind, and therefore is no longer limited to an institution, a locale, or particular educational materials. Christian education is forged and actualized in the struggle for rights, is lived in celebrations of victory, is in pilgrimages reinterpreted in the light of current collective experience, in popular festivals, and so on.

But Christian education, the educational practices of the base communities, has far more important characteristics than these. Christian education is a democratic "space." The group decides its destiny—and proceeds to exercise a new kind of relationship, in total breach with traditional relationships experienced in the churches, in the school, in the factory, and even in the political party (the example cited in our extract).

Here, education shapes a dialectical view of life: all situations and experiences can be seen from two opposing viewpoints—with the eyes of the oppressor or with those of the oppressed.

Education in this context makes possible the reappropriation of the "symbolic capital" of the faith. The people discover, in the popular religious rites and practices used for centuries by the dominant classes to alienate them, the liberative essence of these practices, and their value for the transformation of their own energies into a force for liberation.

Finally, in this new educational practice, the people are experiencing their own capabilities. They are producing a reflection born of action, and not of a new, purely theoretical, system of references that would be foreign to their living reality.

2

Descriptions of Christian Education

The examples that we gave in chapter 1 do not reflect all the practices or all the alternatives of Christian education in Latin America, but neither are they merely anecdotal. They may serve as our starting point for a further step: a search for the scientific tools that will help us to extract all the various elements that constitute the practice of Christian education in Latin America. Before making any attempt to find, in these examples, different models of Christian education, through too empirical and hasty a description, let us consider some different ways of analyzing reality. If we accept that Christian education is a social practice, and not only a theological or a pedagogical one (as we shall demonstrate below), we shall find various focuses and disciplines through which to interpret it, each from its own specificity.

First, it would be legitimate to analyze the various ways of doing Christian education from a *historical perspective,* seeking to locate the genesis of these practices each in a concrete historical context. This would mean a very long investigation, however, were we to undertake it with even a minimal degree of seriousness. Accordingly, we shall not attempt it independently, but only make certain indispensable historical references in the course of our presentation of other approaches. Let us therefore adopt a more generalizing perspective, the *philosophical,* and look for the various philosophical conceptions that are necessarily present in any Christian education project. After all, we must admit that this generally invisible "texture" nevertheless conditions the possibilities and scope of Christian education.

Second, we shall have to take account of the importance of the *political* determination, as we must recognize that this impregnates every Christian education project from start to finish (although not mechanically or absolutely), impeding them or furthering them as the case may be. Third, since we are speaking of Christian education precisely, we shall not be able to understand that without a consideration of the principal models of *pastoral theology* in which the Christian faith is presented in Latin America today. Finally, we shall entertain a brief *pedagogical* description of the various practices of Christian education, inasmuch as the latter pertains to a particular concept of education, and therefore, consciously or unconsciously, makes use of its conceptions and means.

We could go on to list other focuses and disciplines, with long disquisitions on which of them must be the most important or most determining for Christian education. Thus we must wonder, for example, to what degree historical and philosophical determinations are mediated by the economic factor. We shall touch upon this problem, however rapidly, in Part 3. For the moment, our purpose is more limited: we propose to approach the object (Christian education) from various, complementary perspectives, in order to discover the most general models and characteristics of Christian education in Latin America. What we seek to do, then, is to construct a theoretical apparatus that will take the particularities of our object of study in order to interpret and transform it.

PHILOSOPHICAL DESCRIPTION

Let us examine the work of the Brazilian theologian J. B. Libânio. In *Aportes filosófico-culturales* ("Philosophico-Cultural Contributions"), the first volume of his three-volume *Formación de la conciencia crítica* ("Formation of the Critical Conscience"), Libânio offers a simple and concise description of the more significant "mental schemata" implicit in any pastoral practice. Thereby we shall have the wherewithal for a philosophical description of Christian education in Latin America. Libânio's work does not focus specifically on Christian education, but certainly furnishes tools that will fit the object of this study. To attempt to summarize it will be risky, since the result might be too dense and abstract. We shall make the attempt, however, and the utility of doing so will appear in the course of this book.

Libânio precisely delimits the scope of his investigation. He seeks to present a set of tools for the analysis of mental schemata from a point of departure in awareness, and not in historical or structural causality (which does not mean a denial of their relationships).

These mental schemata are defined in function of three "moments" presented in a dialectical succession (but not necessarily a chronological one): Libânio cites the moment of the *object,* that of the *subject,* and that of the *social.* Within each of these three moments, the author considers the human being's fundamental relationships with oneself, with other men and women, with the world and nature, and, finally, with transcendence.

The Object Moment

" 'Object,' here, has the sense of 'thing in itself,' that whose existence is independent of the knowledge that thinking subjects may have of it" (Libânio 1980, 1:30). As for the relation of the subject to itself: in this first moment, the subject perceives itself as unilaterally determined by the object. "All value, all truth, all principle, all good, all law, come from without" (Libânio 1980, 1:31). This mode of knowing is a conformist one. "One's own consciousness of freedom is profoundly marked by obedience to a divine or natural law, external to one's freedom and imposing itself on it" (ibid.).

Human or social phenomena or creations are looked upon as natural or divine manifestations. As there is no consciousness of freedom or autonomy, norms and authorities, considered as external to the awareness, have a great deal of importance. They are the value criteria. This is a mythic mentality, in which human beings and things find their own reality in a participation in a transcendent reality; or else a metaphysical mentality, where human beings understand themselves in dependency on the divine element as source of their own truth and value.

Concerning the relationship of the human being to the self, unless human beings have an awareness of their own worth they will not have any awareness of the worth of others. Here relations among human beings are dictated from without, by laws or morality. Society imposes itself as a ready-made reality. Two categories rule history: fate and divine providence.

Concerning the relationship of the human being to nature in this first moment, human beings live in obedience to the cycle of nature. The natural cycle lords it over all human activities, rather than the human being dominating nature. Nature is the great earth mother, Mother Nature.

As for the relation of the human being to the transcendent in this first moment, the divine world is the sole source of meaning, value, and truth. Human reality has no value in itself.

In this first moment, religion occupies the determining space in human life, embracing all of its areas and bestowing upon them meaning and value. Human experience is sacralized, in function of human beings' perception of their lives as shadowy and insubstantial ontologically. We have a sacralization of time (the "sacred year") and of space (the temple and other sacred places).

In sum, objective elements predominate, and central to them all is orthodoxy. In this schema, "liberation consists in the objective process of the journey through this world of error, ignorance, and falsehood, to right knowledge" (Libânio 1980, 1:49). In this mental schema, that of the "moment of the object," we shall have to conclude that Christian education will consist in the assimilation of a set of objective tenets, whose truth will be measured in terms of their relationship to the divine. In a Christian world, all true education will necessarily be a Christian education.

The Subject Moment

In this second mental schema, the subject plays a decisive role in the very act of the comprehension of the object. Now we have a "negation" of the foregoing moment, in the dialectical sense.

The relationship of the subject to itself is specified in the discovery of subjectivity, understood as "the interiority of awareness as opposed to the exteriority of the world, and revealed precisely as subject of the signification and values by which the human being understands the world" (Libânio 1980, 1:53). The subject perceives itself as source of truth, good, and value. Here, truth is a process resulting from the subject's reflection rather than from without.

Human awareness comes to be distinguished from the world. "Truth is a human reality, not one of things, objects, facts, or occurrences" (ibid.).

The subject has the creative role of interpreting external reality. And so the subject is emancipated: reality is demythologized. An important "anthropological swerve" has occurred: the human being becomes superior to, and takes charge of, reality. This irruption of subjectivity is accompanied by a passion for freedom. Finally, in all of this process lurks the danger of subjectivism, in which the autonomy of certain externals is neglected.

The relationship of the human being with his or her fellows is focused, first, through individualism: the subject, impressed by his or her autonomy and freedom, closes up within the self, in the pursuit of selfish, individualistic interests. "The exploitation of this capacity for individualism occurs especially within the capitalistic economic system" (Libânio 1980, 1:55).

Nevertheless, the discovery of subjectivity may permit the discovery of otherness, of the other. Dialogue, intersubjectivity, *communitarianism* spring up. The other, too, is a source of truth; indeed, truth arises more powerfully in the encounter of subjects. A personalization of human relationships appears, the importance of teamwork, and an emphasis on interpersonal relationships, in which authenticity is now more highly valued than conformity with conventional norms. One seeks a more intimate, personal life, and new, communitarian experiences emerge, even within the church. Human beings come to understand themselves as historical and political beings. They are the real protagonists of history. "In creating history, they create themselves. In creating themselves, they create history as well" (Libânio 1980, 1:57).

As for the relation of the human being to nature: nature comes to be an object of conquest by the reason and will of the human being. Through science, technology, and the perfecting of productive forces, the human being is emancipated from nature. "Human beings begin to understand themselves more and more in relation to work, to a practice calculated to transform the material world and social relations" (Libânio 1980, 1:59).

In the relationship of the human being to the transcendent there is, first, a reaction, in the form of a rejection and denial of transcendency. The human being's autonomous freedom sets itself in opposition to the freedom of God. Atheistic humanisms appear.

There also appears a Christian interpretation of God, against a backdrop of the discovery of subjectivity. Transcendence does not void the autonomy, freedom, and responsibility of the human being; rather, transcendence makes freedom possible and occasions its growth. "Transcendence is the very occasion of the human being's gift to another being. Its rejection, by contrast, is the human being's self-confinement in the tormenting solitude of his or her own 'I' " (Libânio 1980, 1:62).

This mental schema, that of the moment of the subject, entails the danger of subjectivization. The subject, the human being as individual, becomes the sole criterion for the evaluation of any reality.

Christian education is now clearly differentiated from education in general, with a consequent privatization of the former. The validity of Christian education will be measured in function of its "adequacy to the subject" considered individually or as a group, but without attention to the social conditioning of that subject.

The Social (Dialectical) Moment

"As the first synthesis featured the object, and the second the subject, the third synthesis primarily sifts out the actual dialectic of their relationship, thereby transcending the subjectivist nature of the previous moment in a social integration" (Libânio 1980, 1:73). Concerning the relation of the subject to itself, the subject perceives the dialectical nature of its awareness. It thinks, it is the source of value, but it is also thought, and marked by objective structures—those of social conditions.

Human awareness is to be understood as packaged in these three dialectical moments, which subsist in unity but without confusion. It is human beings themselves who are *exteriorized*. Everything that exists in the social world is the creation of the human being. This universe, exteriorized by the human being, is then solidified, *objectivized*; it acquires an existence beyond the consciousness and freedom that have produced it; and it begins to exercise a conditioning, determining activity upon this very subject, with a resulting *interiorization* of the reality of the former on the part of the latter. Then, in turn, this interiorized reality is once more exteriorized and objectivized, in a repetition of the process. The human being's dialectical awareness consists precisely in perceiving himself or herself within this dynamic, this ceaseless process [Libânio 1980, 1:75].

On human beings' relationships with their fellows: now the human being is understood from a point of departure in the social relationships of production and power. The communitarian aspect is insufficient to illuminate the human being's activity; the latter must be situated within its social relationships. All activity has a political dimension. There will be the tendency to overvalue the structural and social element. History is now analyzed in terms of classes, not of individuals. Ideology acquires an importance as the rationalization of the interests of social classes. Ideology plays the double role of the revelation and the concealment of interests.

Concerning the relationship of the human being to nature, one discovers the limits and perils of an irrational, arrogant overmastering of nature. The sort of development by which we are presently being swept along leads to self-destruction.

Regarding the relationship of the human being to the transcendent: in a victory over the denial reaction with respect to the transcendent, in which science is the solitary weapon of understanding, and in which the human being and all that exists are seen as totally characterized by need and decay, there arises a theology of the social, having different forms and seeking to understand God in the process of the transformation of society.

Now God is understood in, and from within, the praxis of liberation, and this gives that praxis its radical sense and eschatological scope. In this mental schema, that of the social moment, faith is "deprivatized," acquiring a political dimension, as its ideological utilization in behalf of dominant interests is unmasked.

The activity of Christian education, like any other Christian or social practice, now comes under suspicion of ideological manipulation. It must be reinterpreted, reformulated in its public and political meaning within social reality.

We are now engaged in a continuous critical process vis-à-vis the dogmatic security of the first moment, constantly on the alert lest, lurking beneath it, there may be elements of influence independent of the subject; and the same with respect to the euphoria of the free, creative subject, as we seek to unmask the social interests that dominate that subject.

Accordingly, this is an extremely critical moment, marked by an awareness of the fact that objectivity is something to be sought after, as it never presents itself in a static state [Libânio 1980, 1:83].

The concept of praxis will now acquire decisive importance in Christian education. The principal criterion of the latter is no longer orthodoxy (as in the first moment) or the simple intentionality of human actions (as in the second). "Theory moves into a second moment. Now theory is considered much more as an 'intelligence of practice' than as an antecedent, abstract, and self-judging principle" (Libânio 1980, 1:85).

In concluding his presentation, Libânio insists that the third moment, or "mental schema," is not the last word, not a finished product. In other words Libânio's analysis is open to history and to new ways of distinguishing the relationships and resolving the conflicts of the human and the social.

POLITICAL DESCRIPTION

In the following paragraphs we shall attempt another characterization of Christian education, using a less generalizing approach than the one just completed, but in no way at odds with it. Here we shall refer to Giulio Girardi's two-volume *Educación integradora, educación liberadora* ("Integrating Education vs. Liberative Education"), with special attention to volume 2, *Cristianismo integrador y cristianismo liberador en la educación* ("Integrating Christianity and Liberative Christianity in Education").

Girardi's thesis is that nowhere in the pedagogical debate is the basic problem a pedagogical one; ultimately the basic problem is one of acceptance or rejection of the capitalist system, that is, it is a problem of political and class option. Inasmuch as education is always inscribed within a project of the human being and of society, there will always be a choice between an "integrating" education, the project of the dominant classes, which seeks to incorporate or to integrate the prevailing system, and a liberative education in the hands of the oppressed classes, who will be seeking liberation from the regime in question. This, according to Girardi, is the basic option for all education. His own polemical statement of the thesis is that "the basic problems of pedagogy are not pedagogical problems," they are political problems. (Of course, this is not to deny the additional importance of specifically pedagogical problems.)

If we admit that Christian education is part of education in general, and if we follow the preceding logic, we are led to assert that what differentiates the various models or practices of Christian education are not religious elements but secular ones.

"The ultimate reference is to the model of the human being and of society which one or another group pursues under the label of 'Christian education.' The basic problems of Christian education are not Christian problems, but human ones" (Girardi, 2:8). We might quarrel with Girardi over his opposition of the human to the Christian, an opposition that will be difficult to reconcile with the Christology being developed in Latin America today. But the author's point is that the political and anthropological option emerging from a class option is more basic than a "religious," or doctrinal, option. This has particular relevance in the present ecumenical debate, both among the various forms of Christian expression and between believers and nonbelievers.

Within this purview, Girardi emphasizes the impossibility of political neutrality in Christian education. His purpose is not to analyze Christian education from what it, or the church, claims that it is, but from the antagonistic, conflicting interests at work in society. "The crisis in Christian education is primarily the function not of the crisis of Christianity, but of that of society, of which Christianity forms an 'integral' part" (Girardi 2:6).

Christian education, however, cannot be analyzed apart from Christianity-across-the-board, which in its globalism has itself always comprised an educational moment. The issue, then, will be where, among the three models that Christianity has assumed and continues to assume throughout history, Christian education will take its position.

And so Girardi attempts to analyze, in this single, complex process, three models of Christianity, corresponding to three projects of the human being and of society: (1) a Constantinian Christianity, preferably linked to the absolute monarchy of a precapitalist society; (2) a liberal Christianity (a secularized Christianity linked to a liberal capitalist democracy); (3) a revolutionary Christianity, linked to a socialistic project. Girardi insists that the relationship between Christianity and these three different production models, respectively, is not mechanical, but enjoys a certain autonomy.

With each of the three models, Girardi analyzes the relationship between the spiritual and the temporal—between the sacred and the profane—with the anthropological, ecclesiological, political, and pedagogical implications of this relationship. Here, very succinctly, are the chief of these implications, with special attention to the pedagogical ones.

Constantinian Christianity

Other authors have examined "Christendom" for the essential elements of this alliance between throne and altar—"Christian civilization," in which religion is accorded the primacy in all areas of this particular type of social organization. We may summarize the main points as follows:

1. The primacy of the spiritual is clearly maintained. The profane is subject to the sacred, and "religious" solutions are everywhere sought. Hence we have a Christian social teaching, a Christian politics, a Christian morality, and so on.

2. An ecclesiocentric view of history prevails. The interests of the church correspond to those of God and of the state. The kingdom of God is realized in the church.

3. There is an irreducible conflict between the church and the world, so that the former must avoid all real contact with the latter.

4. As Christianity is inseparable from authoritarianism, the Christian is a person of law and order.

5. Christianity contributes to the formation of the "good citizen," of whom a powerful state has need and who has need of a powerful state. This is the function of Christianity's pedagogy. "Christian education" appears on the scene.

Pedagogical Implications

Constantinian Christianity is an authoritarian educational movement. It trains men and women to adapt themselves to an absolutist regime. "Education comes to be ruled by the 'demands of the faith,' even though this takes place in the profane area, where Christian education is considered to be the vehicle of specific solutions to specific problems" (Girardi, 2:27).

The meaning of education is summed up in infant baptism. Christian schools spring up, for the defense of the faith against the world by an extension of the protective, authoritarian Christian atmosphere of the family into all of society. Christian education and the "practice of one's religion" become obligatory.

Liberal Christianity

The reason for the expression "liberal Christianity" is that the manifestation of a secularized Christianity has such close ties with capitalist industrialization and its cultural consequences in the nations of the center. In Latin America one must speak of "secularization" with great caution. The points to note here include:

1. Profane reality is recognized for its autonomous dynamism and value—not, however, implying the overthrow of the primacy of the spiritual. The battle for freedom renews Christianity, but without any questioning of the capitalist system.

2. The church recognizes the autonomy of the world (and of the state), abandoning its "Christendom project" and opening up to dialogue. Nevertheless it puts a great deal of resistance to the autonomy of the profane when it comes to analysis—psychological, institutional, or religious.

3. And yet the impulse of the sciences gives rise to the primacy of the temporal as an epistemological principle, which "calls for a study of religious realities (church, theology, Bible, religious experience, sacramental practice) from a profane, scientific, and philosophical viewpoint, with the expectation that the theological viewpoint will take up the conclusion of this study" (Girardi, 2:35).

4. This freedom proclaimed by liberal Christianity, besides not being practiced within the church itself, is objectively negated by capitalist relations of exploitation and domination.

Pedagogical Implications

In liberal Christianity the idea of a mission of education on the part of the church varies in function of the demands of freedom of conscience. The Christian school loses its specificity. Frequently it is not Christian motives (Christian training, for example) that incline parents to send their children to religious schools, but expectations of another kind—better teaching, prestige, a moral atmosphere, a spirit of "law and order," and so on. "Christian education, then, willy-nilly, is only a particular type of profane education, whose 'Christian' character is a secondary determination. It is at the level of this project that the true problem is to be located, and that the radical divergences are concealed" (Girardi, 2:41).

Revolutionary Christianity

Girardi conducts his line of reasoning in the European context, and from a point of departure in the debate, both practical and political, between Christians and atheistic Marxists. Many of the expressions of this debate do not have the same resonance in Latin America, where the Christian-religious factor still plays a salient role, and where the people who are the agents of history are believers.

We shall therefore focus specifically on the pedagogical implications of the changes of a revolutionary Christianity, and thus prescind from the other implications cited in Girardi's investigation.

Pedagogical Implications

Christian education is no longer perceived primarily as an interpersonal relationship having its referent in childhood and youth. Now it is primarily viewed as a movement by which the exploited classes, in their struggle for an alternative society, build a new culture and engender the new human being.

As an active factor in this process, and accepting all of the consequences for faith that flow from this process, Christian education becomes liberative [Girardi, 2:45].

Christian education, whose basic dimension is now the battle for political liberation, is first and foremost a movement of liberation, construction, and the new collective awareness.

It is at the heart of the political struggle, with everything that that struggle involves, that the Christian will discover the traits of his or her authentic formation: the experience of the universality of revolution, the choice for the poor, the demand for personalization, the dialectic of love, and revolutionary radicalization. These exigencies, while not peculiar to Christians, must be present in a liberative Christian education. Furthermore, the primacy of political liberation does not imply a reduction of Christian education to this liberation.

> Faith in the risen Christ, as we have said, is not a "religious" experience in any parochial sense, but tends to be a liberative historical force. To be sure, this faith is rendered a matter of urgency by anthropological and political options; but it reacts upon these, in turn, and is transformed into a source of liberative dynamism [Girardi, 2:65].

A liberative Christian education springs from, and at the same time forms, a liberative Christian community. "In this process, the church is at once liberator and liberated, educator and educated, teaching and learning" (Girardi, 2:72).

Now one can identify the agents and the battlefronts of a liberative Christian education: "The agents of a liberative Christian education are ultimately the popular classes themselves, through their more 'conscientized' sectors, constituted by activists—especially through groups seeking to live their faith at the heart of their political practice" (Girardi, 2:86). All of the points at which oppressed classes and peoples struggle for their liberation are the battlefronts of a liberative Christian education. A liberative Christian education will have specific tasks, such as, for example, the struggle with religious alienation, the discussion in progress within the scholarly and ideological milieu generally, and the liturgy or the manner of information and communication within the church.

DESCRIPTION IN TERMS OF PASTORAL THEOLOGY

The foregoing two approaches, the philosophical and the political, which are complementary (as we shall show in the next chapter), do not exhaust the wealth and complexity of prevailing practices of Christian education in Latin America.

Behind every concrete form of Christian education stands a determinate theology. Reciprocally, to every theology there corresponds a determinate manner of understanding and practicing Christian education. Without going too far afield and attempting to analyze the situation of Christian education in every possible theological system, we shall now examine three approaches, which, while not succeeding one another chronologically, enjoy a relationship with the descriptions we have already seen.

We shall sketch, rapidly, three theological "horizons" against which various Christian-education projects take shape, and in which the Christian faith is taken, respectively, as doctrine, religious practice, and evangelical practice.

Educating for Doctrine

Christian education is customarily understood as the teaching of Christian doctrine, or the transmission of certain fixed, indisputable propositions concerning God, Jesus, the church, the Bible, the Christian life, morality, and so on.

The Church takes care that this transmission be kept within the strict bounds of theological orthodoxy that it has defined. That is, it exercises a zealous control over the teaching of Christian doctrine for the purpose of avoiding deviations that might modify the body of established truths. What is deemed crucial here is that the Christian internalize a precise knowledge of what he or she is to believe, and understand very clearly that each Christian's subsequent behavior is on his or her own conscience. Thus Christians are created with a minimum of intellectual baggage, but without a lived, convinced experience of their faith.

This system is ineffective today, as may be seen in many religious schools. Nevertheless, it will be helpful to this study to observe which theological propositions underlie it. The teaching of Christian doctrine has its point of departure in faith considered as a closed cognitional system. It is a system that is impermeable to the human being, who cannot modify it, and it is closed off from life and history, which fail to penetrate it, and closed even to the message and practice of Jesus, which are transformed, in alienating fashion, into eternal, absolute truths. Faith is not considered as a personal or collective encounter of the human being with God supposing a following of Jesus in love and in the reinterpretation of his message for today.

Above and beyond the series of great dogmatic truths it may convey, this education is the vehicle of an ideology, whose purpose resides in the reinforcement and reproduction of the ecclesiastical apparatus considered as an institution of divine right. Hence this education, often unconsciously, hands on a traditional, conformist view of society, and tends to justify and accept that society, especially in the victims of the organization in question, with all of the hunger and misery it causes. Rather than educating in the faith, one educates in the ideology of the system.

Educating for Religious Practice

Many of those who receive the first type of Christian education that we have examined assimilate a Christian ideology but are not practicing Christians. But more recent emphasis is on educating for religious practice, with its religious functions. What will be the underlying theology of this kind of Christian education?

Religious practice is always an ambivalent phenomenon, frequently the victim of a confusion between the human being's relationship with God and the mediations utilized in this relationship. One grows accustomed to confusing the end with the means. There is the danger of magnifying and sacralizing these mediations and, further, of understanding them outside history and outside their social conditions. The denunciations of false worship by the prophets and by Jesus show to a certain extent just where and how this occurs: there cannot be religious practice or a genuine relationship with God without a practice of justice. This is the difference between faith and idolatry. The theology underlying this education for religious practice often serves to prop up human deceitfulness and to support the manipulation of the religious: a great deal is said about God, but at bottom no respect is shown for the mystery of transcendence, which is manipulated and reduced to ritual. This theology of "signs" often fails of a radical reference to the Other, of an acceptance of a critique by that Other of one's life and society.

Instead the reference is to self-satisfying practices shut up in the religious sphere.

Educating for Evangelical Praxis

Christian education can be an education in Jesus' discipleship. This is effected through a shared experience with others, through a community experience of historical transformation. Here, Christian education is lived and practiced in the following of Jesus, that is, in the service of society's "least ones." Indeed, it is these poor, these oppressed, these nonpersons who become the agents of Christian education, inasmuch as, in their acceptance of the free gift of the kingdom of God, they transform this world of death and chains into a new society of liberty and life.

Christian education assumes a twin attitude of solidarity with the oppressed and denunciation and transformation of situations that provoke injustice. In other words, Christian education takes up an evangelical praxis. The process is precisely a collective one. Like Abraham, like the people of God in the wilderness, like Jesus on his way to Jerusalem, like Paul on the road to Damascus, the people of Latin America are a people on a journey, and therefore they refuse to accept any absolute, powerful, established institution consecrated to the maintenance of an "order" incompatible with the demands of the kingdom of justice and life.

PEDAGOGICAL DESCRIPTION

These descriptions of Christian education would be incomplete if they did not include the pedagogical focus. As with each of the foregoing panoramas, it is evident that underlying each practice of Christian education is a determinate theoretical conceptualization—this time, a pedagogical one—that exerts a significant influence.

In this first, general approach we shall not dwell on an analysis of all prevailing pedagogical systems and projects. Instead, we shall pass quickly from description to interpretation. To this purpose, let us consider three pedagogical alternatives underlying various practices of Christian education: an individualistic education, a personalized education, and a popular education.

Individualistic Education

One of the more evident contradictions in an individualistic type of education is that it is both individualistic and de-individualizing. It is individualistic because it transpires between a learner and an "educator" (that may be a person, a book, a means of social communication, and so on): the learner learns by exactly and literally following the instructions of the educator. At the same time, this type of education is de-individualizing inasmuch as it seeks to force all learners into the same mold, ignoring personal, social, or cultural differences.

This type of education is nearly always in the hands of the dominant classes, who use it to ensure their own survival. Its patterns of behavior and knowledge, then, will be those of the formation of the bourgeois individual. Its basic approach will be the memorization of a store of preestablished truths, and thus it will transmit the baggage that constitutes the "knowledge capital" requisite for the climb to an advantageous position in society.

The most typical example of this type of education is the capitalist school as a selective, ideological apparatus for the training of a labor force (its economic function) and the transmission of the dominant culture (its ideological function).

It should not be forgotten that, although this type of education serves as the most frequent model for Christian education today, it is also selective, and prepares the believer to assume various positions in the ecclesiastical apparatus; and furthermore that it is "reproductive," as it ensures the acceptance not only of Christian values and truths, but also of the structural and institutional forms under which these values and truths are presented.

Personalized Education

Countless efforts are afoot for the modernization and reform of the individualistic, school-based educational system. The basic aim of all of these efforts is a better functional relationship between the educational apparatus in question and modern society. Some projects are so sophisticated and refined that they truly give the impression of fostering radical, in-depth change. At this point a new type of education appears, with two special emphases: one on psychology and the other on educational technology.

The function of psychology in this new educational approach is to differentiate among the various stages in human development. Learning does not occur along a continuum, according to a regular, rectilinear progression, but through a process of trial and error—"two steps forward and one step back." Thus the educator must respect each individual's own development, permitting everyone to study and to learn at his or her own pace. The point is to train a person who will be responsible, active, and independent. No longer is it a question of trying to fit everyone into the same mold. It is a matter of facilitating the growth of capabilities inherent in each individual.

The emphasis on educational technology springs from the effort to impose rationality on, and render profitable, all institutions of an advanced industrialized society, which cannot afford the tremendous discrepancy in traditional schooling between investment and end result. Here the point is to identify the mechanisms of learning that will make for a maximal use of time and effort through a maximal rationality in their procedures. This type of education, stressing now the psychological, now the technological, envisions a liberal ideal of the human being, without questioning the social structure as a whole.

Group-learning experiments may be conducted, divorced from the old individualism. These will be encouraged if they are seen as more effective and personalizing. But the group will never come to grips with the structure of the world to which it belongs, since it will not have the tools with which to do so.

Here Christian education will place a great deal of emphasis on the importance of interpersonal relationships and group dynamics. The community constitutes the privileged space of learning, but what appears in relationships among persons here is only the absolutized intersubjectivity of the components of the group. What is created is but a new island, seemingly protected from social conditions.

Popular Education

Popular education seeks to break free of the two basic conditions of the types of education already described: it does not limit itself to a school setting, and it endeavors to remain independent of manipulation by the dominant ideology. As to the first aspect: popular education recognizes that human beings are not educated exclusively in school. All human activities are in some way formative, especially work as transformative of nature. Education is no longer an individualistic or personalized task, but is basically collective: it is a social practice born of human relationships mediated by the world.

The second aspect, that of nonmanipulation by the dominant ideology, surely implies a more difficult, broader undertaking. Here we have not just an idealistic wish, a mere longing for a different society but, rather, the actual radical transformation of present society and the creation of a new culture springing from this process of social change. An organized people, engaged upon the process of winning its freedom and building a new society, becomes the agent of its own education.

Christian popular education is a process of "accompanying the people," of reinterpreting the people's Christian practice and experience from a point of departure in the liberative experience of faith as a collective adventure of active response in the building of the kingdom of life. (We shall return to the subject of Christian education and popular education in chap. 11, below.)

3

Principal Models of Christian Education

In chapter 2, through a number of different lenses, we examined the single reality of the diversity of Christian educational practices in Latin America today. We saw that the various analytical tools that could be applied to an analysis of this reality—philosophical, political, theological, and pedagogical—are reciprocally complementary. Their vectors intersect; they enjoy common outlooks. In virtue of these intersections, we here propose to reorder the material under our scrutiny and present these educational practices synthetically.

In this fashion, in view of what has been said up to this point, we arrive at three objective models of Christian educational practice ("objective" because we prescind from what Christian education actually intends to be or do in each model). Thus we have a *spiritualistic,* a *liberal*, and a *liberative* model of Christian education (see table, pp. 38–39). These three models correspond in part to three historical moments, three distinct human projects in the history of the church and society. But, as we saw in chapter 1, they also belong to our present reality, and still maintain conflict-ridden relationships in that reality.

We may say, then, that this classification, which we shall synopsize later, takes account not only of the evolution of Christian education in time (the "diachronic perspective"), but also of its situation at the present moment (the "synchronic perspective").

MODELS OF CHRISTIAN EDUCATION

	Economic	*Philosophical*	*Political*
		Objective	*Constantinian Christianity*
Spiritualistic Christian Education	Feudalism	Determined by the object (divine reality) Human being's submission Religion as the source of truth Juridical elements Orthodoxy	Christendom Primacy of the spiritual Service to the church Authoritarianism Infant baptism Defense of the faith Education = Christian education
		Subjective	*Liberal Christianity*
Liberative Christian Education	Capitalism	Autonomy and subjectivity of the subject Truth in function of the subject Demystification Anthropological bent Privatization and compartmentalism of Christian education Radicality, human freedom	Autonomy of the profane Primacy of the temporal Freedom of conscience Acceptance of capitalism Findings of science
		Dialectical	*Revolutionary Christianity*
Liberal Christian Education	Historical Project of the People (Self-managed Socialism)	Thinking and thought subject Social integration The subject within relationships of production and power Political dimension of faith Orthopraxis	Building a new awareness by exploited classes Battle for political liberation Church as educator and learner Educating agent = an organized people Struggle with religious alienation

Theological	*Pedagogical*
Doctrine	Individualism
Transmission of dogma Orthodoxy Faith = cognition of indisputable truths Faith = ideology	De-individualization Development of an individual in function of authoritarian society Memory School system Selection, reproduction

Religious Practice	*Personalism*
Personal, lived experience of faith Ritual Communitarian experience without social commitment	Modernizing, reformist Development of the person More effective education Group dynamics

Evangelical Praxis	*Popular Education*
Following of Jesus by the poor Building of the kingdom Collective training Reading of the historical facts and deeds of liberation	Education in praxis Creation of a new culture by the people Accompaniment of the people

SPIRITUALISTIC CHRISTIAN EDUCATION

We have selected this name for the first model that we propose to consider because it seems to us to convey a notion of the great dichotomies maintained by this model, such as faith and world, church and politics, soul and body, and individual and society. In each of these dichotomies, emphasizing the first half is emphasized and extolled at the expense of the latter part.

1. Spiritualistic Christian education is intimately bound up with a feudal type of economic structure in which the dominant class is composed of large property owners.

2. Spiritualistic Christian education is connected to a mental schema corresponding to the moment of the "object." That is, it is totally determined by the object understood as divine reality or faith, and considered as essentially foreign to and distinct from the human being as subject. Spiritualistic Christian education seeks to inculcate an attitude of total submissiveness in human beings' relationship to the divinity, inasmuch as the religious sphere is seen as the determining instance and sole font of truth and value. Here Christian education stresses the juridical and the orthodox.

3. Spiritualistic Christian education is linked to a Constantinian conceptualization of Christianity—that is, to a Christendom. Here the spiritual enjoys primacy over the temporal in such wise that human and social content loses its interest. Christian education is at the absolute service of the church, and fosters an ecclesiocentric view of the world in which the church is the already realized kingdom of God. The first and principal sign of this model of Christian education is infant baptism, and its principal task is the "defense of the faith." Any education, in order to be genuine education, must be Christian.

4. Spiritualistic Christian education is linked to doctrine, the strict transmission of dogma. It receives its identity from orthodoxy, and preserves it in virtue of a confusion of faith with the assimilation of predetermined, indisputable knowledge and truth. Faith is an ideology. The elements constituting it are bound up with a determinate class, however unconsciously, and seek to legitimate this particular social formation.

5. Spiritualistic Christian education, in its pedagogical manifes-

tations, is at once individualistic and de-individualizing. It seeks not the development of the person or group, but the conformity of an individual's functions with an authoritarian society. Memory takes precedence over reasoning. This model is identifiable with the school model, together with its selective, reproductive options.

LIBERAL CHRISTIAN EDUCATION

By comparison with the model just examined, liberal Christian education provides for a relative emancipation of the individual and a greater respect for the person. Hence its qualification as "liberal." Its naïve or voluntary ignorance of social conditions issues in the maintenance and propagation of an illusion: the proclamation of liberty, equality, and fraternity in the framework of a social structure that requires oppression, competition, and inequality in order to exist and grow.

1. Liberal Christian education is bound up with the economic structure of capitalism, with the private ownership of the means of production, and with a capitalist division of labor and knowledge. By capitalism we mean the industrial capitalism of the nations of the center as well as the dependent and backward capitalism established in Latin America.

2. Liberal Christian education is linked to a "subjective" mental schema, that is, to the subject's acquisition of an awareness of his or her autonomy and subjectivity or agency. This subject is basically the one who has solved the problem of his or her material needs.

The truths of Christian education are measured by the yardstick of the subject. There is an attempt to demythologize certain values and truths, involving a considerable anthropological swerve in the direction of a general subjectivization of reality, and this phenomenon is manifested both in an individualism and in a communitarianism.

A liberal Christian education encounters God in intersubjectivity, and in the radicality of human freedom. It becomes privatized and compartmentalized; that is, it no longer pretends to address the entire field of education.

3. Liberal Christian education is bound up with liberal Christianity, which sponsors not only the autonomy of the profane and

temporal, but its primacy. Here Christian education divests itself of its authoritarian quality and respects freedom of conscience, although this freedom has no connection with the freedom denied by the capitalist structure. Christian education gives up its dogmatic, triumphalist, conquistadorian quality and takes account of the findings of science.

4. Liberal Christian education is linked to an appreciation and rediscovery of religious practice, in which the subject has not merely a knowledge of the faith, but a living, personal experience of it through ritual. Christian education undertakes the task of facilitating the relationship of human beings with God, and comes to confuse the end with the means. Christian education is limited to community religious practices, without the community taking on a real role of service in the world.

5. Liberal Christian education is closely linked to a personalized, modernizing, reformist pedagogy. It values the development of the person, in respect for his or her own characteristics, and seeks a more agreeable, effective form of education. Christian education here is lived within a "group dynamics," where the internal mechanisms are read from a point of departure in persons, not in social conflicts considered to be foreign to the group.

LIBERATIVE CHRISTIAN EDUCATION

"Liberative Christian education" refers to a Christian education that takes up and promotes a liberation that is understood in all the radicality and breadth of the term: liberation as the change of social, economic, mental, and faith structures, and so on, and liberation that is not just a dream, but one that the Latin American people battle for in struggle and in martyrdom.

1. Liberative Christian education is linked to the building of a new society and a new economic structure. Girardi cites "autogestionary socialism." We shall use no such labels, and shall speak of the historical project of a people who envisage, first, the defense of life and an equitable distribution of goods.

2. Liberative Christian education is situated within a dialectical mental scheme, in which the subject is at once "thinking" and "thought," free of social conditions and determined by them. Christian education here cannot be addressed to the individual

apart from his or her social group, or without taking account of the social relationships of production and power. The political dimension of faith is essential to liberative Christian education, whose criterion is a conformity not with an orthodoxy but with an orthopraxis—that is, with a transformative social practice consistent with the Christian message of liberation.

3. Liberative Christian education is bound up with a new model of Christianity whose traits still remain to be identified. It is linked to the construction of a new culture by the exploited classes. The basic content of liberative Christian education is the battle for political liberation.

The church is at once educator and educand, and an organized people is the principal educating agent. The principal task of the people as educator will be part of the ideological struggle in general, and will consist in the struggle with religious alienation.

4. Liberative Christian education will be defined as evangelical praxis: the following of Jesus will be lived in solidarity with the poor and in the transformation of the situation that lies at the root of poverty. Liberative Christian education is motivated by, and is an active response to, the challenge of the upbuilding of the kingdom. Hence it is a collective formation, and a reading of the historical deeds and facts of liberation from a point of departure in faith.

5. Liberative Christian education is a popular education, an education in a praxis linked to the creation of a new culture and beginning in the struggles of which the people constitute the agency. Liberative Christian education, then, is an "accompaniment of the people."

PART 2

CHRISTIAN EDUCATION
IN THE LIGHT OF THE WORD

In this second part of this book we shall attempt to bring the reality of Christian education in Latin America into confrontation with the biblical message. More precisely, we shall ask whether the Bible in its educational dimension provides any criteria for an option among the three models of Christian education that we have discovered.

The reality of Christian education, analyzed in the light of a scientific instrumentality, must now enter into dialogue with the word of God. The dialogue will be reciprocal. We shall endeavor to read the word of God from the reality of Christian education in Latin America. At the same time, we shall endeavor to interpret and to transform that reality in the light of the Bible.

Clearly the models of Christian education that we have examined rest on a determinate, specific use of the Bible in respect of its educational message. But we are also convinced that the Bible has certain educational axes that do not lend themselves to arbitrary interpretation or manipulation. What we propose to do, then, is not to deduce a Christian educational theory from the Bible, but to bring reality and project, conditions and values into mutual confrontation.

4

Hermeneutic Principles for an Analysis
of Education in the Bible

There are insuperable, unconcealable differences in the distance that yawns between the Bible and ourselves. The Scriptures belong not only to a different age, but also to different modes of production, different societal organizations, different cultures, institutions, mentalities, and so on.

No wonder, then, that differences and even contradictions appear in descriptive or evaluative comparisons between biblical educational practices and those described above—that is, in a discussion of a phenomenon as historically and culturally determined as education. No judgment can be passed on education in the long-ago days of the Bible without taking account of this historical and cultural distance with all that it implies.

Nevertheless, a comparison between educational practices proper to such diverse moments will not be without its utility and legitimacy. After all, although the Bible and its conceptual world are far removed from the circumstances here and now, the Bible has a characteristic of transcendent import for the Latin American people: it was written by and for a poor people. Beyond all the social, linguistic, and cultural differences, a bridge spans the ages and the miles: the language of the oppressed in their glimpse of a liberation at the end of their tunnel; and along the journey through the darkness of the tunnel, education has a role to play, and some inspiring to do.

It can be ambiguous and even dangerous to speak of "the Bible" as a homogeneous unity, as if it were a manual from which one might extract norms and doctrines relating to certain themes and sets of problems. The question "What does the Bible have to say about education?" is captious. It supposes that the Bible, like a good encyclopedia, will have a single, always explicit, conception of education. Anyone with even a superficial acquaintance with the broad, complex process of the formation of the books of the Bible in the process of their coming together and being reworked as our Bible knows that this cannot be the case. Throughout the twelve centuries of the written composition of the Bible (several centuries of oral tradition), we find, successively or simultaneously, various pedagogical projects, with constant breaches in terms of advance and retreat.

Thus the Bible, here as elsewhere, has no monolithic shape. But we need not go to the other extreme, and consider each separate book, or even the parts of a book, to sponsor totally original theological or educational outlooks, and thus abandon all hope of discovering a sense of unity, a sense of the whole, so important in biblical interpretation. Modern scientific exegesis often succumbs to this latter temptation.

Lest we fall into either extreme—exaggerated unity or absolute diversity in what the Bible posits regarding this subject—let us recognize that there are various vectors in the Bible, reflecting the advances and gains as well as the failures in which the people of God lived historically. If we believe in the continuity of the people of God, and in God's fidelity in historical processes, these vectors will help us to interpret the educational situation through which the people of Latin America are moving. Our undertaking, then, will be hermeneutic rather than exegetical.

By way of hypothesis, let us posit that the various educational projects appearing throughout the Bible, despite their contradictions, enjoy ultimate articulation, centering upon a particular axis or its negation. This axis might be formulated as follows: God's people come to know God, as well as themselves, in the historical processes of liberation in which their destiny of freedom comes to be.

Theologians customarily encounter a danger when they approach the Bible. They do so from the limited outlook of their discipline and interests, thereby neglecting other, most promising points of departure, such as a sociological, anthropological, or, as in our case, pedagogical outlook.

The theologian then proceeds to ask what the Bible has to say about education. But if we look at the Bible more closely as a cultural phenomenon and literary product, we see at once that the Bible itself originates and develops typically as a pedagogical project. The Bible *is* education, whether it talks about education or not.

The whole point of consigning the word to writing is to be able to teach that word with more force and continuity, to be able to hand on and reactualize an educational historical event—not to write up a list of educational norms. The Bible, then, is the *result* of an educational process. This broadens our task. In order to establish a correct relationship between the Bible and Christian education, it will not be enough to search out a few biblical passages that talk about education. We shall have to understand the pedagogical dynamics with which the whole of the Scriptures are shot through, seeing that these Scriptures were written with an interest so clearly pedagogical.

It is meaningless to speak of Christian education when we read the Old Testament, for example—and not only because it does not directly speak of Christ, but basically because we generally use the expression "Christian education" with the assumption that there is some neat difference between Christian education and just plain education. In the Semitic mentality and culture (still very present in the New Testament as well) there is no line of demarcation between what we would call religious education and what we would call education. Religion invades all areas of knowledge and life experience.

Once again, therefore, it is very important not to try to analyze the educational problematic by projecting our own cultural presuppositions. For us, and for the division of knowledge so peculiar to the prevailing ideology, knowledge or teaching about health, nutrition, civics, and so on will be radically different from religious knowledge or teaching. By contrast, the Hebrew mind very readily integrates and globalizes all of these things.

Further, for many centuries the intellectual element was not divided from the existential, the historical, or the spiritual. These separations were introduced specifically by Greek philosophy, which displaced and radically transformed Jewish culture in all of its manifestations, especially where education is concerned.

5

Education in the Old Testament: The Agents

METHODOLOGICAL PRINCIPLES

As we have already suggested, there are several approaches available for the investigation of the subject of education in the Old Testament. A first possibility would be to follow the historical development of Israel, and thereby to see how education occurred in each of a series of decisive historical stages: the origins of Israel, the exodus, the settlement in Canaan, the time of the kings, the exile, the return, and so on. But we are not equipped for such an approach, nor would it answer to our objective.

A second possible approach would consist in an analysis of certain books and authors of the Old Testament in which education has a particular relevance: Deuteronomy, Jeremiah, Proverbs, and so on. The difficulty with this route is that we would have no historical, theological, or pedagogical guidelines to follow.

A third possibility would be to search for a synthesis of the broad approaches to education throughout the whole of the Old Testament, looking, for example, for certain key terms. This is the method followed by theological dictionaries of the Bible, a method that sometimes loses sight of the historical dimension.

We shall search for, and propose, a more pedagogical approach, seeking to identify who were the educators, the "educational agents," in Israel in the course of history, and what were the principal characteristics of their pedagogy.

TWO CONSTANTS IN OLD TESTAMENT EDUCATION

We find, in the historical development of education in Israel, a theological constant and, in all of its structural and institutional forms, a sociological constant. The theological constant is that God is considered to be the principal and authentic educator. The sociological constant is that the family is the essential, absolutely basic educational institution in Israel. Against this background, various educational models arise, successively or simultaneously, along with their respective secondary educational agents.

A God Who Educates

Israel, in its various professions of faith, constantly refers to God as its instructor or educator, regardless of what particular form or organization of education currently prevails.

O God, you have taught me from my youth,
   and till the present I proclaim your wondrous deeds
                                        [Ps. 71:17].

Teach me to do your will,
   for you are my God.
May your good spirit guide me
   on level ground [Ps. 143:10].

This teaching, which the prayers of the psalmist represent as imparted directly by God to the believer, actually has a number of distinct historical manifestations and mediations.

Before going into further detail, let us make an observation about vocabulary that will help us to understand the educational problematic that runs all the way through the Old Testament. Many passages in which "instruct," "teach," or even "guide" occur in translations are actually using the noun *musar*, from the Hebrew root *YSR*, with the principal meaning of "correction," "castigation." *Musar* can refer to corporal punishment, by means of the "rod" (Prov. 22:15), or to a "chastisement" by word, to correction. In the latter sense it can be broadened still further and no longer refer so much to correction properly so called, but to what we call education. This is the sense in which the "punishments" of Jeremiah 10:24 are to be understood: "Punish us, O Lord, but with equity, not in anger, lest you have us dwindle away."

God's correction-education of the people is effected in various manners. First, it may be through historical events of liberation. In the following text, four events occur as part of God's pedagogy: the plagues on Egypt (v. 3), the miracle of the sea (v. 4), the passage through the wilderness (v. 5), and the punishment of the rebels. (v. 6).

It is not your children, who have not known it from experience, but you yourselves who must now understand the discipline of the Lord, your God; his majesty, his strong hand and outstretched arm; the signs and deeds he wrought among the Egyptians, on Pharaoh, king of Egypt, and on all his land; what he did to the Egyptian army and to their horses and chariots, engulfing them in the water of the Red Sea as they pursued you, and bringing ruin upon them even to this day; what he did for you in the desert until you arrived in this place; and what he did to the Reubenites Dathan and Abiram, sons of Eliab, when the ground opened its mouth and swallowed them up out of the midst of Israel, with their families and tents and every living thing that belonged to them. With your own eyes you have seen these great deeds that the Lord has done [Deut. 11:2–7].

Second, God may exercise the act of corrective education through divine law, in the inarticulate voice of thunder, in the words of the commandments handed down by Moses:

Out of the heavens he let you hear his voice to discipline you; on earth he let you see his great fire, and you heard him speaking out of the fire [Deut. 4:36].

Or again, the Lord may teach through destruction. It would seem that after having exhausted all possible resources, and every political, intellectual, and spiritual action, there is nothing left but destruction to make a people react when they are unwilling to assume and actualize their destiny of freedom.

> . . . This city has excited my anger and wrath, so that I must put it out of my sight for all the wickedness the Israelites and Judeans, with their kings and their princes, their priests and their prophets, the men of Judah and the citizens of Jerusalem, have done to provoke me. They turned their backs to me, not their faces; though I kept teaching them, they would not listen to my correction [Jer. 32:31–33].

Finally, the pedagogy of correction with which God teaches the people, after the foregoing three forms of education, arrives at its term. Now instruction will no longer be necessary. God will reveal the divine self to the people completely:

> But this is the covenant which I will make with the house of Israel after those days, says the Lord. I will place my law within them, and write it upon their hearts; I will be their God, and they shall be my people. No longer will they have need to teach their friends and kinsmen how to know the Lord. All, from least to greatest, shall know me, says the Lord . . . [Jer. 31:33–34].

We should not forget another way that the Old Testament has of describing God's educational process with the people (and this will bring us to the section of this chapter relating to family education). God educates the people as a parent educates a child.

> Remember how for forty years now the Lord, your God, has directed all your journeying in the desert, so as to test you by affliction and find out whether or not it was your intention to keep his commandments. He therefore let you be afflicted with hunger, and then fed you with manna, a food unknown to you and your fathers, in order to show you that not by bread alone does man live, but by every word that comes forth from the mouth of the Lord. The clothing did not fall from you in tatters, nor did your feet swell these forty years. So you must realize that the Lord, your God, disciplines you even as a man disciplines his son [Deut. 8:2–5].

When Israel was a child I loved him,
    out of Egypt I called my son.
The more I called them,
    the farther they went from me,
Sacrificing to the Baals
    and burning incense to idols.
Yet it was I who taught Ephraim to walk,
    who took them in my arms;
I drew them with human cords,
    with bands of love.
I fostered them like one
    who raises an infant to his cheeks;
Yet, though I stooped to feed my child,
    they did not know that I was their healer [Hos. 11:1–4].

Family Education

Throughout the Old Testament the family is the educational institution par excellence, not only in that its function as such is seen in all eras and all stages of the life of Israel, but also because there is nothing to take its place as an educational institution except the synagogue, whose appearance was much later. Without the family's contribution to education, Israel's continuity, as well as its fidelity to its traditions over the centuries, is inexplicable. The father of a family is responsible for his children's education. If they are male, he will hand on to them his office and the traditions of his people. The mother has the same task: "Hear, my son, your father's instruction, and reject not your mother's teaching" (Prov. 1:8).

The concern here is for an "elementary" education, in which the essential elements of the faith are taught. This is moral, liturgical, and historical education, recalling the origin and meaning of Israel's great solemnity, the Passover sacrifice, the rite of the Unleavened Bread.

When your children ask you, "What does this rite of yours mean?" you shall reply, "This is the Passover sacrifice of the Lord, who passed over the houses of the Israelites in Egypt . . ." [Exod. 12:26–27].

On this day you shall explain to your son, "This is because of what the Lord did for me when I came out of Egypt." It shall be as a sign on your hand and as a reminder on your forehead; thus the law of the Lord will ever be on your lips, because with a strong hand the Lord brought you out of Egypt . . . [Exod. 13:8–9].

We could multiply our examples of passages that we meet in an unequivocally pedagogical context, where the literary device is one of dialogue between teacher and pupil within the family: "When your children ask you. . . ."

What is peculiar to Hebrew education is the transmission of a particular word, then: "With a strong hand the Lord brought [us] out of Egypt. . . ." Unlike neighboring peoples, with whom ethnic or religious "belonging" was manifested through tattooing, or by wearing certain objects, Israel's distinctive "mark" was the "word" of the people's historical liberation. "Let this, then, be as a sign on your hand and as a pendant on your forehead: with a strong hand the Lord brought us out of Egypt" (Exod. 13: 16).

The didactic question will refer not only to rites, ceremonies, and commandments, but to monuments as well: "When your children ask you: What do these stones mean?" the father, in reply, will narrate the historical event of the crossing of the Jordan and the arrival in the Promised Land.

All of these questions refer to the father's instruction of his children in the Israelite profession of faith:

. . . When your son asks you what these ordinances, statutes and decrees mean which the Lord, our God, has enjoined on you, you shall say to your son, "We were once slaves of Pharaoh in Egypt, but the Lord brought us out of Egypt with his strong hand. . . . Therefore, the Lord commanded us to observe all of these statutes in fear of the Lord, our God, that we may always have as prosperous and happy a life as we have today; and our justice before the Lord, our God, is to consist in carefully observing all these commandments he has enjoined on us" [Deut. 6:20–25].

Parents likewise teach their children poems or songs (for example, the Song of Moses [Deut. 32:1–43]), which will have a precise pedagogical function, and not only a liturgical or popular mnemonic one vis-à-vis the acts and deeds of liberation. They will actually provide a criterion and a yardstick for the practice of the people:

> ". . . Write out this song, then, for yourselves. Teach it to the Israelites and have them recite it, so that this song may be a witness for me against the Israelites. For when I have brought them into the land flowing with milk and honey which I promised on oath to their fathers, and they have eaten their fill and grown fat, if they turn to other gods and serve them, despising me and breaking my covenant; then, when many evils and troubles befall them, this song, which their descendants will not have forgotten to recite, will bear witness against them. . . ." So Moses wrote this song that same day, and he taught it to the Israelites [Deut. 31:19–22].

The "rod" is of special importance in the upbringing of children. "He who spares his rod hates his son, but he who loves him takes care to chastise him" (Prov. 13:24). "The rod of correction gives wisdom, but a boy left to his whims disgraces his mother" (Prov. 29:15).

THE PEOPLE EDUCATE THE PEOPLE

As we know, at least eight centuries elapsed between the actual adventures of Abraham and the first written records of those events. Similarly, more than two hundred years intervened between the actual exodus event and its first written redaction at the court of King Solomon.

All through the years preceding the composition of the written records of these events, the people of Israel educated themselves regarding them, thanks to a collective memory, or what historians of the Old Testament call "oral tradition."

For generation after generation, the events at the origin of the existence of the people of Israel—ultimately God's interventions in their history—were transmitted orally. Education and history were closely intertwined throughout this entire phase. On the one hand, history was the basic content of the Israelites' self-education; on the other hand, this education guaranteed the continuity, reinterpretation, and actualization of history.

This was education for living. This God who was to be made known, whose actions for freedom were to be handed on from generation to generation, was the God of life, the one who had bestowed upon Israel liberty and the land, which were capsulized in the rich concept of "salvation."

Education, then, sought to "accompany" and deepen this liberation process, and to keep it from "getting off the track," one might say. Such an education will necessarily be a community endeavor, and its purpose will be the strengthening of a people for the task of responding to their destiny of freedom.

It is true that we have no written evidence of this era. It is probable, however, that the celebrated professions of faith that we find in the books of Deuteronomy and Exodus, which constitute the earliest texts in the Bible, sprang up in the course of this process of oral tradition.

THE PROPHETS: THE EDUCATING WORD

A study of the phenomenon of prophecy from a specifically educational viewpoint could open new doors and provide a great stimulus for Christian education today in Latin America. The prophets are not formal or traditional educators. They have no systematized or even orderly teachings to transmit. They probably stand at the antipodes of what we today would call educational technique.

The prophets are charismatic teachers in the best sense. No institution can control them or, indeed, further their efforts. Today they will be at the royal court, tomorrow with the priests. Nearly always they will be with the people (but certainly not to flatter them). Never do we find them "teaching a class." They are forever catching people by surprise.

One thing is sure: the prophet has absolutely no "control of the material," as we demand of a pedagogue today. On the contrary, the prophet is dominated and possessed by what is to be taught or preached. The prophet is an instrument of the *dabar Yahweh*, the word of Yahweh.

> Indeed, the Lord God does nothing
>   without revealing his plan
>   to his servants, the prophets.
> The lion roars—
>   who will not be afraid!
> The Lord God speaks—
>   who will not prophesy! [Amos 3:7-8].

Prophecy is an uncontrollable demand made on the prophet, one that the prophet cannot ignore.

The prophet enjoys almost total autonomy vis-à-vis the people constituting the audience. Never does the true prophet seek to please (although the false one does, and this is the difference between the two). The teachings of the true prophet are generally very harsh, disturbing, and radical. As we see in Jeremiah 28, the true prophet, unlike the false, can never preach hope or reconciliation in a situation of sin or injustice. Until there is a radical change in the people, there is no hope for a betterment of their situation, and chastisement and catastrophe are in the offing.

Liberation and salvation do not come cheap. They demand a radical, painful change in persons and in structures. Scarcely, then, will the prophet enjoy popularity. No one likes to listen to such a one. These unpleasant persons will not only denounce the rich, denounce oppressors, but will excoriate as well the mechanisms of oppression that have been internalized by the people—a people who, thanks to their forgetfulness of their history of liberation, become the accomplices of their own subhuman situation. And so the prophet's teachings are resisted and rejected.

> And whether they heed or resist—for they are a rebellious house—they shall know that a prophet has been among them. But as for you, son of man, fear neither them nor their words when they contradict you and reject you, and when you sit on scorpions . . . [But speak my words to them, whether they heed or resist, for they are rebellious.] [Ezek. 2:5-7].

The work of education entails the isolation and often the persecution of the prophet.

> Yes, I hear the whisperings of many:
>   "Terror on every side!
>   Denounce! let us denounce him!"
> All those who were my friends
>   are on the watch for any misstep of mine.
> "Perhaps he will be trapped; then we can prevail,
>   and take our vengeance on him"
>   [Jer. 20:10; (cf. Amos 7:10–17)].

It would be impossible to attempt to synthesize here the teachings of the prophets with respect to content. But we need not neglect their pedagogy, especially their methodology. The prophet is neither a preacher nor an ordinary teacher. The prophet "teaches" in a very particular way: by a combination of word and deed, by question and statement, by direct, concrete example and metaphor.

Let us pause for a moment on one very particular resource utilized by the prophet, a most impressive one: the prophetic sign, also called the "symbolic action." One may manage to ignore the virulence of a prophet's words. One may somehow render them harmless, or simply pay no attention to them. But one cannot do the same with the symbolic action. The latter is so powerful, so provocative, so radically, subversively challenging, that it simply cannot be overlooked. Further: there are never prophetic signs without explanatory words. In the prophetic action, God's word becomes *event*, and a new language appears:

1. In order for the message to "hit home," morality is relegated to secondary consideration. Thus in Hosea 1:2, 3:1, the prophet espouses a prostitute, and has three children by her, in order to demonstrate to the people that the people have become prostitutes, and worse, children of prostitution.
2. Isaiah, by command of the Lord, must walk naked among the people (Isa. 20), in order to proclaim that Egypt represents no hope for Israel and no guarantee of defense against

Assyria—that, on the contrary, in relying on Egypt they shall be standing naked before the aggressor.

3. Ezekiel must act out an imaginary deportation, emerging from his lodgings by night with all of his possessions, digging a hole in the city wall like someone fleeing in utter desperation, and thus dramatizing the inevitable exile and deportation of his people to Babylon (Ezek. 12).

4. Jeremiah performs at least six symbolic actions, of which the most impressive is perhaps the purchase of a plot of ground at a time when the city of Jerusalem is under siege and seemingly without hope of escaping a debacle. Jeremiah buys the plot of ground as a sign of hope, in dramatic anticipation of the days of return and reconstruction (Jer. 32:1–15).

With the prophets, education is not the mere transmission of the traditions or "truths" of a people. It is not simply the ideological production of determinate historical conditions. With the prophets, education becomes eminently creative, and even "gets the upper hand on history," one might say. Any modern educator, Christian or not, might well envy the prophet's power to blaze new trails for history, by remaining faithful to a pedagogy open to the word of judgment and liberation.

THE PRIESTS: EDUCATION BY THE TORAH

The word *torah*, usually translated "law," comes from a root meaning "to point out," "to teach." A *torah*, then, will be a lesson, an instruction.

The Torah is very peculiarly and directly linked to the priesthood. Originally, a *torah* was a brief instruction on some particular point or problem, some practical rule of conduct, especially for the celebration of worship, which was the specialty of the priest. It was the priest who had to decide between the sacred and the profane, the clean and the unclean, and who then instructed the faithful accordingly.

The Lord said to Aaron [Israel's first priest], "When you are to go to the meeting tent, you and your sons are forbidden under pain of death, by a perpetual ordinance throughout your generations, to drink any wine or strong drink. You must be able to distinguish between what is sacred and what is profane, between what is clean and what is unclean; you must teach the Israelites all the laws that the Lord has given them through Moses" [Lev. 10:8–11].

All of the various specific prescriptions of the law come down in some way from the Torah received by Moses. The priest is the one in charge of the transmission, explanation, and application of the Torah.

When Moses had written down this law, he entrusted it to the levitical priests who carry the ark of the covenant of the Lord, and to all the elders of Israel, giving them this order: "On the feast of Booths, at the prescribed time in the year of relaxation which comes at the end of every seven-year period, when all Israel goes to appear before the Lord, your God, in the place which he chooses, you shall read this law aloud in the presence of all Israel. Assemble the people—men, women, and children, as well as the aliens who live in your communities—that they may hear it and learn it, and so fear the Lord, your God, and carefully observe all the words of this law. Their children also, who do not know it yet, must hear it and learn it, that they too may fear the Lord, your God, as long as you live on the land which you will cross the Jordan to occupy [Deut. 31:9–13].

It is true that the education imparted by the priests tends to reproduce or apply a set of values and body of knowledge having a restricted base. But the addressees are the whole people. At no time is the audience restricted to an elite.

Teaching by the priests is intimately bound up with an institution, the Temple, especially after the experience of the exile. Now education is formalized and restricted, in view of the urgency of preserving culture and faith in the presence of so influential a foreign civilization. Still, the teaching role of the priest is not strictly limited to the casuistic application of the law within the narrow framework of the Temple. His responsibility involves taking serious account of the global situation in which the people live, and of how justice is practiced or neglected in their social relationships.

> [Hear the word of the Lord. . . .]
> "But let no one protest, let no one complain;
>   with you is my grievance, O priests!
> You shall stumble in the day,
>   and the prophets shall stumble with you at night. . . .
> Since you have rejected knowledge,
>   I will reject you from my priesthood;
> Since you have ignored the law of your God,
>   I will also ignore your sons . . ." [Hos. 4:4–6].

COUNSELS OF THE WISE: EDUCATION FOR LIVING

The "wise," the possessors of wisdom, were educators whose function varied through the centuries. At first, owing to Egyptian influences, they were connected with the court, and it was their duty to "give the king good advice." But the wisdom movement is broader and more complex than this, and includes a profoundly popular component. The teaching of the wise, then, may be divided into a popular wisdom and an elitist pedagogy.

By "wisdom" Israel understood a practical knowledge of the laws of life and of the universe, based on experience. The Hebrew word means, first, skill—the practical experience of something. In the teachings of the wise there is a close relationship between education and experience. Their proverbs are the fruit of experience, and the generalizations they make eschew any abstraction. They set forth an "art of living" for the solution of the problems of the everyday.

The teaching of the wise is concerned with the integral character of life as a single unit. It always begins with facts, never with theories. It is an open teaching, rectifiable in function of new discoveries. Using modern categories, we might say that it is an inductive type of knowledge and teaching. It is an education that never tires of relating the life of a human being to nature or, rather, to all the experiences that this human being may have at the level of the concrete things that shape the context and milieu of living. Let us not forget, of course, that a *concept* of nature was altogether foreign to the Hebrew mentality, which never dealt in the abstract.

To be sure, all of these teachings presuppose knowledge of and faith in Yahweh. "The fear of the Lord is the beginning of knowledge; wisdom and instruction fools despise" (Prov. 1:7).

The research carried out by the wise and transmitted to their pupils is limited to the defense of life, without pretensions of entering into the field of metaphysics: "In his mind a man plans his course, but the Lord directs his steps" (Prov. 16:9).

> There is no wisdom, no understanding,
>   no counsel, against the Lord.
> The horse is equipped for the day of battle,
>   but victory is the Lord's [Prov. 21:30–31].

The struggle of the wise is with "foolishness," which we must not understand merely as an intellectual or moral defect. "Foolishness" is a kind of behavior, a disorder at the human being's vital center. Since the proper activity of the teacher of wisdom is counsel and advice, the term used for education is, once more, *musar*, which appears no less than thirty times in the book of Proverbs alone. It can be considered synonymous with prudence and wisdom. The counsel "Get the truth, and sell it not—wisdom, instruction and understanding" (Prov. 23:23) is complemented by the one that reads, "Listen to counsel and receive instruction, that you may eventually become wise" (Prov. 19:20).

Musar is a pathway to life:

> For the bidding is a lamp, and the teaching a light,
>   and a way to life are the reproofs of discipline . . .
>   [Prov. 6:23].

> A path to life is his who heeds admonition,
>   but he who disregards reproof goes astray [Prov. 10:17].

When all is said and done, the effect of *musar* is life. We are dealing with education for living:

> So now, O children, listen to me;
>   instruction and wisdom do not reject!
> Happy the man who obeys me,
>   and happy those who keep my ways,

Happy the man watching daily at my gates,
  waiting at my doorposts;
For he who finds me finds life,
  and wins favor from the Lord;
But he who misses me harms himself;
  all who hate me love death [Prov. 8:32–36].

Finally, the method of the wise one is molded in various uses of language: wisdom, popular sayings, advice, and enigmas. The content of the teaching of the wise may be natural science, law, pedagogy, or theology.

THE SCRIBES: TOWARD A SCHOOL EDUCATION

In the course of the second century B.C., there arose a group of persons called "scribes," who were considered to be the successors of Ezra, and who also had a connection with the priesthood. ". . . This Ezra came up from Babylon. He was a scribe, well-versed in the law of Moses which was given by the Lord . . ." (Ezra 7:6).

The scribes were to become the inspiration of various other groups that soon formed: Sadducees, Pharisees, and Essenes. The emergence of this new class of educators was an outgrowth of contact and struggle with Hellenism. The ancient doctrine of the priests no longer sufficed for the maintenance of the teaching of the law. New techniques, introduced by the Greeks, had to be used, new approaches to interpretation, and updated pedagogical resources.

The scribes, whose duty it was to safeguard tradition and explain and apply Scripture, were also called "doctors of the law," or "rabbis." Their specialty was juridical questions. One became a scribe not by virtue of one's social origin or because one's father had been one, but through long and deep study, and a lengthy apprenticeship in the home of a teacher. This study consisted primarily in repeating what the teacher had said until it became engraved on the mind. Teacher and pupil held long "dialogues," with an ordered succession of questions and answers.

This same era saw the rise of the synagogue, a religious and educational institution that had begun perhaps as early as the exile, but more probably had its origins in the Egyptian diaspora. The synagogue was not a place for celebration of the ritual sacrifice, which was reserved for the Temple. The synagogue was the place where the community gathered to pray and to be taught the law. It became the center of community life, where community affairs were discussed and conducted.

The principle of strict reservation of sacrifice to the Temple necessitated the creation of centers of teaching and celebration everywhere. The liturgy celebrated in the synagogue was rigidly prescribed, and itself had a great deal to do with the interpretation of the Torah, or Pentateuch (in Aramaic translation, since the people no longer understood Hebrew), and the prophets. Preaching, generally in the form of a simple paraphrase of the text, might be done by any male member of the community.

It is very difficult to determine the exact date of the appearance of the actual school that came to be conducted in the synagogue. A class might be held in the same space used for the liturgical celebration, or the location might be different. A teacher would initiate his pupils into the reading and interpretation of the law. Alongside this "elementary education" were also more advanced studies, and "grades" began to appear. Boys would enroll in the synagogue school at six or seven years of age. Girls remained under the instruction of their mothers.

IN CONCLUSION

Undeniably, the pedagogical wealth of the Old Testament, despite enormous cultural differences separating that world from the present-day Latin American reality, will be a source of very deep inspiration and challenge for Latin America's own pedagogical practices and educational models.

The most evident general characteristic of Old Testament pedagogy is that it is nearly always a pedagogy of popular education: (1) It is handed down by an oral tradition whose vehicle is the popular memory. (2) The pedagogical method of the prophets is a popular one, a subversive one, questioning the status quo and combining a criticism of the oppressors with a self-criticism of the oppressed. (3) Education at the hands of the priests is popular—of the people— being conducted through the popular celebration of the historical facts and deeds of liberation, and through the systematic recall of the laws laid down in favor of life. (4) The education conducted by the wise ones is one of popular wisdom—knowing how to live and how to act, a wisdom forged by the people themselves through their concrete experiences.

It would be a serious mistake, however, to idealize the historical reality of Old Testament education. Some of its methods are most distasteful, based as they are on violent repression. There are disadvantageous structural forms in the educational organization of the Old Testament, such as that of the synagogue, whose educators were devoted to an ideological, conservative task rather than to one of renewal and liberation. Indeed, all the forms of education and all the educational agents and agencies that we have cited are under a cloud of ambivalence: they can just as well serve the further repression of the people as their liberation. The only constantly faithful educator in the Old Testament is God.

Thus the Old Testament recounts not only education's successes, but also its failures: the chosen people stumble constantly, make mistakes, wander away from the historical project that God has traced for them. "Come," they said, "let us contrive a plot against Jeremiah. It will not mean the loss of instruction from the priests, nor of counsel from the wise, nor of messages from the prophets. And so, let us destroy him by his own tongue; let us carefully note his every word" (Jer. 18:18).

As we see, then, educational agencies of whatever sort may lend themselves to a "taming" sort of education.

> Her leaders render judgment for a bribe,
> > her priests give decisions for a salary,
> > her prophets divine for money . . . [Mic. 3:11].

> Prophetic vision shall fade; instruction shall be lacking to the priest, and counsel to the elders . . . [Ezek. 7:26].

On the basis of everything that has been said above, and without forgetting the diversity of educational practices in the Old Testament, including their negative effects, we may say that, on balance, the educational project of the Old Testament is clearly liberative and popular.

6

Jesus as Teacher

Any attempt to distinguish the pedagogical activities of Jesus from those of the first Christian communities is difficult and risky. Here we have the great problem of the historical Jesus and the post-Easter or post-Paschal Jesus, coupled with the near impossibility of knowing Jesus of Nazareth except through the testimonials of faith handed on to us by his followers. Nevertheless, for methodological reasons, let us consider the teaching ministry of Jesus apart from that of his disciples and the church. In this chapter we shall endeavor to do a pedagogical reading of Jesus' ministry, keeping in mind the Latin American reality and educational practice.

JESUS TEACHES

Only the synoptic Gospels use the verb *didaskein* ("to teach," "to instruct"), but the word occurs there some one hundred times, generally with reference to the activity of Jesus.

Whom does Jesus teach? Generally speaking, Jesus teaches the "crowds," that is, the people, his disciples, certain groups at hand, individuals, or the people's religious leaders.

Where does Jesus teach? Jesus teaches in the synagogues, in the Temple, but mostly in the open air, in villages, on the seashore, along the roads.

What is the point of departure of Jesus' teaching? Jesus makes constant use of the Old Testament in his teaching. He also uses nature and the world around him, taking concrete, material examples from his surroundings, both natural phenomena and the specific customs of his age and culture. Often he makes use of the concrete existential situation in which his hearers live.

How does Jesus teach? The forms and techniques of Jesus' teaching are varied and are adapted to circumstance. We have dialogue and encounters, parables, figures of rhetoric (proverbs, paradoxes, irony, repetition, and so on), questions, and a great number of other techniques.

WAS JESUS A RABBI?

Jesus' pedagogical practice can be understood only against a background of the great Old Testament educational currents. The Gospel accounts show us various persons approaching Jesus and calling him "Rabbi." Let us see how Jesus is like the rabbis and how he differs from them.

In many respects, Jesus is like the rabbis:

1. Like the rabbis, Jesus has a group of disciples with whom he has close ties.

2. Like them, Jesus preaches and teaches in the synagogue, debating with his adversaries. He is asked questions about doctrine, and is even asked to resolve purely juridical problems, such as the matter of an inheritance: "Someone in the crowd said to him, 'Teacher, tell my brother to give me my share of our inheritance.' He replied, 'Friend, who has set me up as your judge or arbiter?' " (Lk. 12:13–14).

3. Jesus' manner of teaching does not seem to have broken with that used by the doctors of Israel in whose company he could be found during his youth: "On the third day they came upon him in the temple sitting in the midst of the teachers, listening to them and asking them questions" (Lk. 2:46). The rabbis were experts in the art and technique of dialogue.

4. Like the scribes, Jesus makes numerous references to biblical texts, and comments on them.

He came to Nazareth where he had been reared, and entering the synagogue on the sabbath as he was in the habit of doing, he stood up to do the reading. . . . Rolling up the scroll he gave it back to the assistant and sat down. All in the synagogue had their eyes fixed on him. Then he began by saying to them, "Today this Scripture passage is fulfilled in your hearing" [Lk. 4:16, 20–21].

5. Finally, as we have mentioned, Jesus is called a teacher by the people, by his disciples, and by the scribes themselves (Mk. 9:17, 38; Lk. 10:25; etc.).

Still, there are definite differences between Jesus and the doctors of the law, especially the following:

1. Jesus teaches everywhere.

2. Jesus teaches every class of persons, especially those condemned and rejected by Jewish law—women and children, publicans, fishers, the sick, prostitutes, and all manner of "unclean" persons.

3. Jesus prefers a pedagogical style not to be found in the rabbinic literature, that of the parable.

4. The relationship Jesus maintains with his disciples is different from that between a rabbi and his pupils. Jesus' disciples are called, rather than their joining him on their own initiative or for the purpose of starting out on a career; they receive no instruction in the law; their status as disciples is not a temporary one, to last only until they become teachers themselves. "No pupil outranks his teacher, no slave his master. The pupil should be glad to become like his teacher, the slave like his master" (Mt. 10:24–25).

5. Jesus' approach to the interpretation of the ancient texts is clearly different from that of the rabbis. Jesus does a rereading of the passages of the Old Testament from a point of departure in his own practice, without utilizing them as a universal, absolute norm.

6. The controversies on tradition in Matthew show clearly that Jesus is breaking with "the tradition of the ancients," that is, from the set of commentaries on the law handed down in the rabbinical schools. "Pharisees and scribes from Jerusalem approached Jesus with the question: 'Why do your disciples act contrary to the tradition of our ancestors? They do not wash their hands, for example, before eating a meal' " (Mt. 15:1–2).

7. Jesus is a popular teacher, whose authority attracts attention. "Jesus finished this discourse and left the crowds spellbound at his teaching. The reason was that he taught with authority and not like their scribes" (Mt. 7:28–29). Jesus' authority does not come

through the same channels of training as that of the rabbis; rather, he is of humble origin, which surprises and scandalizes people:

> Jesus next went to his native place and spent his time teaching them in their synagogue. They were filled with amazement, and said to one another, "Where did this man get such wisdom and miraculous powers? Isn't this the carpenter's son? Isn't Mary known to be his mother . . . ? . . . Where did he get all this?" [Mt. 13:54–56].

In sum, we may state that in teaching on God, God's kingdom, and God's will, Jesus does not depart very far from the received themes of contemporary Judaism. What is different is his treatment of that content: he radicalizes it in defense of the life of the people, as over against abstract theories used in an ideological fashion to maintain a particular religious and social structure.

THE CONTENT OF JESUS' TEACHING:
THE KINGDOM

The principal novelty in Jesus' preaching and teaching, as compared with the currents of the age, are to be found in his treatment of the kingdom of God. The subject itself is not a new one, but Jesus invests it with new content. Judaism professes a kingdom of God that will extend, for the present, only to Israel, but that will be recognized by all nations at the end of the ages. Jesus uses the concept of kingdom in this same eschatological sense, but never in that of a permanent reign of God over Israel in the present. The novelty of Jesus' concept of the kingdom of God is that for him this kingdom has already been inaugurated in all its dimensions, and that its present manifestations are such as these: "Go and report to John what you have seen and heard. The blind recover their sight, cripples walk, lepers are cured, the deaf hear, dead men are raised to life, and the poor have the good news preached to them. Blest is that man who finds no stumbling block in me" (Lk. 7:22–23).

The socially dead, like the all but physically dead, live once more. Life irrupts into the midst of suffering and death. The time of salvation has begun. Jesus makes use of familiar biblical symbols to express this reality: light, the harvest, a fig tree. As we shall see, he teaches not only in words but in deeds.

Jesus' teaching on the kingdom, then, is that it is at once eschatological and present. He portrays the kingdom both as a gift freely
given by God and as a present demand for transforming action.

The kingdom implies judgments upon reality, and changes in
that reality. To teach the kingdom is to teach that justice and those
changes. Hugo Echegaray puts it in this way: "Thus the proclamation of the kingdom focuses on the universal action of God in favor
of the poorest and sees in this action a manifestation of his transcendence. This means that the reign of God cannot be identified
with the plans and policies of the kingdoms of this world, which
pay little attention to 'the oppressed of the earth' " (Echegaray
1984, p. 80).

Jesus' teaching resumes one of the central notions of the Old
Testament—that the sovereignty of God is manifested in history, in
God's identification with the weakest of the weak. Further, Jesus
includes himself in the object of his teaching, "In my opinion, the
originality of Jesus consists in his connecting the signs of the
kingdom with his own person and in his radicalizing its demands
but at the same time developing them with reference to their
foundation in God, thus exercising a creative fidelity to the spirit of
the Old Testament" (Echegaray 1984, p. 81).

Jesus' teachings, and especially his message with respect to the
kingdom, are profoundly theocentric. For example, the Beatitudes
make no attempt to identify who the poor (or the poor in spirit) are.
They seek only to indicate who God is and what God's kingdom is
like. This they do by speaking of the poor, not because the poor
have any merit of their own, but because they are the victims of an
unjust society, and because God, in the divine kingdom, wishes to
reestablish justice.

Jesus resumes the prophetical tradition, particularly in its insistence on the unconditional relationship of the gift and advent of the
kingdom to the poor in history's present. We must not overlook
that the passage we have cited from Luke, and Jesus' actual pro-
grammatic discourse in the synagogue in which he sums up his
educational project, are quotations from Isaiah:

> The spirit of the Lord is upon me;
>   therefore, he has anointed me.
> He has sent me to bring glad tidings to the poor,
>   to proclaim liberty to captives,

Recovery of sight to the blind
and release to prisoners,
To announce a year of favor from the Lord
[Lk. 4:18–19; see Isa. 61:1–2].

Jesus pointedly distances himself from the religious groups of his age with his conception of the kingdom, and very especially from the scribes and the Pharisees. For these, propheticism had died forever, its place usurped by a commentary on the law that reduced the kingdom to a moral, individualistic abstraction, devoid of any effect on history or society.

Here we have a clear picture of a confrontation between two models of education: the one creative, globalizing, and transforming, the other conservative and ideologizing.

DEED AND WORD: AN EDUCATIONAL PRACTICE

Jesus draws a great deal of inspiration from the pedagogical method of the prophets, especially from the symbolic action. As we shall see, his symbols refer directly to the kingdom and its demand for liberation.

> The contribution of Jesus was to restore the prophetic perspective in the context of present circumstances and to see the latter in the light of the promises and blessings of the kingdom. This he did in his preaching but also by means of various symbolic actions: healings, exorcisms, the expulsion of the merchants from the temple, his table fellowship with the poor and with sinners, his offer of forgiveness, and so on. By means of this "indirect" type of speaking Jesus made the kingdom a vehicle for the revelation of God; . . . Above all, the kingdom manifests with disconcerting power the love, justice, and goodness of the Father [Echegaray 1984, p. 84].

The excellence of Jesus' pedagogy does not reside solely in the rhetorical resources employed by him, or even in the content and message he communicates. His pedagogy is well-rounded indeed. His symbolic actions are not used simply to reinforce the words of a statement. Rather, the whole of his practice has a pedagogical scope: it is an integral, liberative practice, going far beyond discourse.

Jesus' liberative actions seek once more to reveal who his Father is and what project that Father has in view for human beings. Word and deed are intimately connected in these actions; and anyone failing to grasp the word will likewise fail to understand the deed, just as anyone not seeing and drawing profit from the deed will likewise have no understanding of the word. This is why Jesus' actions and teachings are so simple, and so easily grasped by the simple, without the need for any recourse to the complicated speculations of the scribes.

> The reader will recall, for example, how the "Jews" ask Jesus for heavenly signs comparable to the exodus miracles of the distant past. Jesus offers them, as signs of the kingdom, a series of liberating actions that attend to the elementary needs of human beings. His adversaries reject these because they have a pre-established and almost magical idea of how God's power should manifest itself. In the eyes of Jesus, however, the manifestation of divine power should be measured by the concrete and therefore less striking needs of the poor rather than by the hunger for wonders that is cultivated by those whose basic needs have already been satisfied.
>
> In Jesus' conception of the kingdom the sense of God is thus accompanied by a sensitivity to the poor brother and sister [Echegaray 1984, p. 85].

But Jesus' option for the poor is no simple demagoguery, bereft of any real commitment to them or their cause. Nor is it an ascetical process. And certainly it is not an idealization of poverty. It is a visible, didactic sign of a sharing-in-solidarity with the poor, and of a struggle against poverty.

> In this sense Jesus does not explicitly offer a doctrine of God that he himself has exclusively developed. Rather, he speaks constantly of God in an indirect manner; basically, he is continually developing the theme of the kingdom in proclamatory actions and words. The kingdom comes not to ex-

plain the world but to transform it; it comes to human beings in order to reveal the Father to them, that is, to reveal the God who makes them the object and aim of his love and who is therefore a power that does away with all the conditions preventing full human growth [Echegaray 1984, p. 88].

This union of deed and word, this accommodation of the intent, action, and discourse, is far more than the invention of an educational genius who teaches by means of his example and his existence. It is beyond the reach of the ordinary person, being rooted in the mystery of the person of Jesus as principal protagonist of the kingdom and as incarnation of the God of life. The solidity of Jesus' authority issues from his service to the cause of the "least ones," and not from the complicated orthodoxy of a theoretical or moralistic argument.

As we have said, Jesus' practice was integrally pedagogical. It combined the two constitutive aspects of all education: transmission and creativity. His practice was not bounded by any specific institution or formality. Jesus does not even follow a formal teaching plan. He educates by drawing on all of the natural, social, and existential events by which his hearers are surrounded.

Furthermore, Jesus' educational practice overflows traditional frontiers and ignores the divisions of knowledge and of social activity. His educational practice is likewise unambiguously "economic," in that it deals with material life, with the production and circulation of goods.

One cannot teach a kingdom whose special concern is for the concrete needs of the oppressed in one's society (in the case of Jesus an imperial society constructed on the amassing of goods, on exclusive wealth, on indebtedness as a tool for the reinforcement of relations of dependency, and on scarcity of material goods for the great masses) without proposing a change in the organization of that society. For Jesus, the task of a liberative, popular education proceeds necessarily by way of a liberation from the economic structures of domination.

An exchange of spiritual goods becomes an ideological facade if there is no material exchange. Here we are at the heart of the logic of gift and communion with the poor that Jesus teaches and practices. A reciprocity in the circulation of material and spiritual goods is essential:

". . . Give, and it shall be given to you. Good measure pressed down, shaken together, running over, will they pour into the fold of your garment. For the measure you measure with will be measured back to you" [Lk. 6:38].

". . . A good man produces goodness from the good in his heart; an evil man produces evil out of his store of evil. Each man speaks from his heart's abundance" [Lk. 6:45].

The logic of the kingdom is the logic of superabundance promoted and shared. The logic of empire is that of the indebtedness that subjects and humiliates.

Nor can one teach a kingdom signifying a new organization, a new way of living in society, without proposing a radical change at the political level. Faced with the politics of empire, which is based on domination, competition, stratifying division, violence, abuse of power, and the like, the logic of the kigdom will have the shape of a diakonia to the masses, of equality, and of power based on justice and service.

"You know how among the Gentiles those who seem to exercise authority lord it over them; their great ones make their importance felt. It cannot be like that with you. Anyone among you who aspires to greatness must serve the rest; whoever wants to rank first among you must serve the needs of all. The Son of Man has not come to be served but to serve—to give his life in ransom for the many" [Mk. 10:42–45].

Finally, Jesus' integral educational practice radically questions the religious and ideological structure synthesized in the structure of the Temple. The teaching of the kingdom "destroys" the Temple conceived as a political center that justifies class divisions, as an economic center of the collection and distribution of surplus labor, and as a religious center of sacrifices and normative, orthodox religious discourse. The functions of the Temple were so interiorized and accepted by the various sectors of the Palestinian population, even by the victims of these functions, that when Jesus attacks this basic ideological structure he loses his popular support. Even the people are astounded by Jesus' popular, liberative education.

THE POOR TEACH

Inasmuch as the poor—the concrete, material poor, the victims of a system of death, and those others who identify with their struggle against poverty—are not only the special addressees of the kingdom but its principal vehicles as well, then we must say that the poor teach to the extent that they adapt themselves to the project of the kingdom and take up the corresponding practice.

We see this with all clarity in various passages in the Gospel, and especially in one of Jesus' prayers: "Father, Lord of heaven and earth, to you I offer praise; for what you have hidden from the learned and the clever you have revealed to the merest children" (Mt. 11:25). The poor, then, teach the kingdom, in receiving the good news, as we have seen in the passage from Luke: "Blest is that man who finds no stumbling block in me" (7:23).

Are we merely propounding a new legalism here? Will truth, will perfect instruction, instead of being found in a book, in a law, in a set of moral norms, now be reduced and closed up within a particular social class? No, this revelation to the poor, this revelation of which the poor are the privileged vessels and vehicles, is a manifestation of the freedom of God, of the God of life, defender of the oppressed. Matthew's Beatitudes remind us that there is no such thing as the sacralization of a social class as such. No, blessed too are the poor *in spirit*—echoing the whole Old Testament tradition of the *anawim Yahweh,* to be sure, but broadening its sense to include all who have the same humility and availability as the material poor, and who are therefore ready to take up their destiny and calling, materially and spiritually, to abolish poverty, for the triumph of life over death. Here we are at the heart of the concept and practice of popular education conducted by Jesus.

GOD THE SOLE TEACHER

We have already referred to the profoundly theocentric nature of Jesus' preaching. We reemphasize it here to show that this constant insistence of the Old Testament on a God who manifests divine fidelity through education is of the first importance in Jesus' teaching, and hence throughout the New Testament.

We have already cited Jesus' polemic with the teachers of the law. In the Gospel of John—to which we have not referred as yet, as it merits a treatment apart, especially in any pedagogical reading of Jesus' practice—we find a synthesis of the notion of God as sole teacher, complemented, furthermore, by the idea of the poor that we have just considered.

> The feast was half over by the time Jesus went into the temple area and began to teach. The Jews were filled with amazement and said, "How did this man get his education when he had no teacher?" This was Jesus' answer: "My doctrine is not my own; it comes from him who sent me. Any man who chooses to do his will, will know about this doctrine— namely, whether it comes from God or is simply spoken on my own. Whoever speaks on his own is bent on self-glorification. The man who seeks glory for him who sent him is truthful; there is no dishonesty in his heart . . ." [Jn. 7:14–18].

One who seeks not his or her own glory, but God's, is precisely the poor one in the biblical sense of the word—the just one before God, the one who has nothing either materially or spiritually that could make any demands on God.

What Jesus says and does is what God has taught him, and not the application of a new pedagogical method invented by himself. God educates through Jesus, basically by teaching among society's oppressed and exploited. Jesus' pedagogy is a response to the radical demands of liberation that God makes upon the people.

7

The Primitive Church as Educator

The church of the New Testament, like the people of God in the Old, is the subject of a constant dialectical tension between educating and being educated. The church is educated: it does not have its center, its raison d'être, within itself; it is not the possessor of its own truth. At the same time, it educates: it originates from this truth and is entirely dependent upon it and on the fulfillment of its mission to proclaim it.

THE HOLY SPIRIT AS EDUCATOR

Jesus' post-Paschal instruction to his disciples to go forth and teach becomes possible of execution with the coming of the gift of the Holy Spirit. "Full authority has been given to me both in heaven and on earth; go, therefore, and make disciples of all the nations. Baptize them in the name of the Father, and of the Son, and of the Holy Spirit. Teach them to carry out everything I have commanded you, and know that I am with you always, until the end of the world" (Mt. 28:18–20).

The Holy Spirit continues and deepens Jesus' educational undertaking: "This much have I told you while I was still with you; the Paraclete, the Holy Spirit whom the Father will send in my name, will instruct you in everything, and remind you of all that I told you" (Jn. 14:25–26).

The disciples, now become the first Christian community in

Jesus' absence, can rely on his Spirit to remind them of what Jesus used to say and do when it comes to applying it in the present moment. The Spirit is that power and ability to communicate, that new language, which human beings discover on the day of Pentecost. Christian teaching no longer has limits or boundaries.

The teaching activity of the primitive church is of a forthrightly charismatic nature, and furthermore is bound up with the expectation of the imminent coming of the kingdom of God. Hence its call and exhortation to a radical conversion. Given the urgent, spontaneous nature of this education, there is no specific institution that could be its agency, so that the pedagogical agent is the apostle, teaching as part of the global ministry.

We must emphasize once more that the whole process of the formation of the New Testament is the reflection of this intense educational activity. The books of the New Testament, especially the Gospels, were redacted on the basis of the work of preaching and teaching of the first Christian communities.

EDUCATION AND MISSION

Education, for the first church communities, is carried out in function of mission. Indeed it is defined by mission. This mission is the following of Jesus in the prolongation of his practice, and the activity of teaching will therefore be in the footsteps of the pedagogical practice of the Master.

Luke, in Acts, seeks to demonstrate the continuity between the ministry of Jesus and that of the apostles. Like Jesus, they teach in the Temple, the synagogue, or people's homes: ". . . They went into the temple at dawn and resumed their teaching" (Acts 5:21). "Day after day, both in the temple and at home, they never stopped teaching and proclaiming the good news of Jesus the Messiah" (Acts 5:42).

Like the teaching of Jesus, that of the apostles provokes conflicts, and causes the teacher difficulties. The Jewish authorities are taken aback that these "uneducated men of no standing" could speak with such assurance and illustrate their teaching with wonders. The popular education of the apostles collides with the elitist education that has been so well planned by the Jewish authorities:

Observing the self-assurance of Peter and John, and realizing that the speakers were uneducated men of no standing, the questioners were amazed. Then they recognized these men as having been with Jesus. When they saw the man who had been cured standing there with them, they could think of nothing to say. . . . So they called them back and made it clear that under no circumstances were they to speak in the name of Jesus or teach about him [Acts 4:13–14, 18].

The apostles, however, were not intimidated, and continued to teach what they had seen and heard, accepting the risks of their undertaking. " 'We gave you strict orders not to teach about that name, yet you have filled Jerusalem with your teaching and are determined to make us responsible for that man's blood.' . . . They were stung to fury and wanted to kill them" (Acts 5:28, 33).

Despite the repression, the mission moves out very rapidly, throughout the whole Greco-Roman world. The subversive memory of Jesus' practice, which is the heart of all of these teachings, cannot be silenced.

PHASE ONE OF THE PRIMITIVE CHURCH AS EDUCATOR: THE APOSTOLIC TEACHING

As we stated above, the apostles' teaching activity was at first bound up with, and inseparable from, their preaching. It was spontaneous, not institutional, and deeply popular and creative.

The teaching activity of the apostles takes on a number of different complementary aspects, which for methodological reasons we shall now examine separately and in detail. In the concrete, however, we must remember that these aspects are often found interrelated, and even indistinguishable from one another.

A Christian Rereading of the Scriptures

The reinterpretation or rereading of religious tradition in the light of the present situation (which has already played a decisive role in both Old Testament education and Jesus' own pedagogical ministry), and in the light of the actual message of Jesus is basic in the teaching activity of the apostles. Peter's Pentecost discourse is an eloquent example, as also are the descriptions that we find of Paul's teaching methods:

> Following his usual custom, Paul joined the people there and conducted discussions with them about the Scriptures for three sabbaths. He explained many things, showing that the Messiah had to suffer and rise from the dead [Acts 17:2-3].

> The things that happened to [our forebears] serve as an example. They have been written as a warning to us, upon whom the end of the ages has come [1 Cor. 10:11].

Transmission of the Kernel of the Christian Faith (the Kerygma)

In their zeal to continue Jesus' own teaching activities, the apostles seek to hand on what is basic—what is closest to the heart of Jesus' own message. Thus, for example, we have Paul's account of the institution of the Eucharist: "I received from the Lord what I handed on to you, namely, that the Lord Jesus on the night in which he was betrayed took bread . . . " (1 Cor. 11:23).

The basic element of the kerygma that the apostles seek to transmit is capsulized by Paul in one of the oldest passages in the New Testament: "I handed on to you first of all what I myself received, that Christ died for our sins in accordance with the Scriptures; that he was buried and, in accordance with the Scriptures, rose on the third day . . . " (1 Cor. 15:3-4). Paul insists on the authority of this teaching, on its nature as revelation. This is not his own commentary or interpretation. This is the kerygma, which must be handed on just as it is.

Jesus' Statements

Various collections of Jesus' sayings circulated in the first communities, some probably in writing (in documents no longer extant), and the apostles, like the authors of the New Testament, used them to carry out their pedagogical task.

These sayings surely had great didactic value. But with the passage of time, they turned out to be insufficient. Standing alone, apart from the memory of the practice of their author, they eventually called for some kind of commentary, lest they degenerate into abstract discourse.

The Professions of Faith

Many of the professions of faith to be found in the New Testament, formulae of great importance in the apostolic teaching, were composed for the celebration of baptism. This preserved the educational dynamic that relates the word of God with sign, or symbol.

The best known of these professions of faith is probably the one that we find in the letter to the Philippians: "Your attitude must be that of Christ: Though he was in the form of God, he did not deem equality with God something to be grasped at. Rather, he emptied himself and took the form of a slave, being born in the likeness of men. He was known to be of human estate, and it was thus that he humbled himself, obediently accepting even death, death on a cross" (Phil. 2:5–8).

Exhortation

The apostles' teaching also quickly takes on an ethical dimension in its confrontation with the pagan world. The ethical aspect of the apostles' teaching is oriented to adoration and witness (martyrdom).

PHASE TWO OF THE PRIMITIVE CHURCH AS EDUCATOR: THE TEACHING OF DOCTRINE

As the Christian communities continued to develop, the sense of the imminent coming of the kingdom began to wane. The mission went on, but now the life of organized communities, with their new problems, required attention and specific efforts. The Christian movement became less charismatic, and the preservation of the life of the church began to require a certain degree of institutionalization. This is the context of the so-called pastoral (or protocatholic) letters.

The ministry of the apostles, which had previously been conditioned exclusively by preaching and mission, now began to diversify. "The things which you have heard from me through many witnesses you must hand on to trustworthy men who will be able to teach others" (2 Tim. 2:2). Teaching content, which had been inseparably linked to the preaching of the central kerygma, began to have a greater specificity: "These are the things you must teach and preach. Whoever teaches in any other way, not holding to the sound doctrines of our Lord Jesus Christ and the teaching proper to true religion, should be recognized as both conceited and ignorant . . ." (1 Tim. 6:2-3). As we see, the basic Christian message, the kerygma, the kernel and nucleus of the faith that must be stirred up, is now accompanied by a certain doctrine, a deposit of truths reinforcing and developing this principal message.

The pastoral letters frequently cite good or "sound" doctrine, the doctrine faithfully handed on and safeguarded—in other words, taught. "If you put these instructions before the brotherhood you will be a good servant of Christ Jesus, reared in the words of faith and the sound doctrine you have faithfully followed" (1 Tim. 4:6). "As for yourself, let your speech be consistent with sound doctrine" (Tit. 2:1).

Teaching now involves the handing on of a tradition that is fixed, to a point, and has the tendency to stabilize and close in upon itself. The gospel, which always proclaims the new, is now converted into a teaching to be learned, to be received in all its purity, and to be defined against erroneous doctrines. The faith becomes first and foremost fidelity to a body of doctrine, to an official creed and touchstone of orthodoxy. The defensive, conservative side of teaching will be emphasized.

The office of "teacher" *(didaskalos)* appears. The evolution of this ministry is significant. After listing the gifts of the Holy Spirit, Paul enumerates various church offices: "Furthermore, God has set up in the church first apostles, second prophets, third teachers, then miracle workers, healers, assistants, administrators, and those who speak in tongues. Are all apostles? Are all prophets? Do all work miracles or have the gift of healing? . . ." (1 Cor. 12:28-29).

In Paul, as we have said, these functions are not specific or separate. The apostles are primarily missioners sent forth by the community; the prophets are in charge of the homily in the liturgical assembly; and the teachers engage in a more or less methodical teaching activity based on the Scriptures, after the manner of the rabbis.

In the course of time, the function of the *didaskalos* became more precise, and tended to become independent and specific. James's warning to those who coveted the post of teacher, or who held themselves forth as teachers, shows us that by his time this office had been formalized: "Not many of you should become teachers, my brothers; you should realize that those of us who do so will be called to the stricter account. All of us fall short in many respects. If a person is without fault in speech he is a man in the fullest sense, because he can control his entire body" (Jas. 3:1–2). Teachers were probably commissioned by a laying-on of hands as in Judaism.

False teachers are denounced, in the name of the gospel and of the doctrine inspired by the gospel: "I repeat the directions I gave you when I was on my way to Macedonia: stay on in Ephesus in order to warn certain people there against teaching false doctrines and busying themselves with interminable myths and genealogies, which promote idle speculations rather than that training in faith which God requires" (1 Tim. 1:3–4).

The message of the pastoral letters with regard to education is summed up in the second letter to Timothy:

> In the presence of God and of Christ Jesus, who is coming to judge the living and the dead, and by his appearing and his kingly power, I charge you to preach the word, to stay with this task whether convenient or inconvenient—correcting, reproving, appealing—constantly teaching and never losing patience. For the time will come when people will not tolerate sound doctrine, but, following their own desires, will surround themselves with teachers who tickle their ears. They will stop listening to the truth and will wander off to fables [2 Tim. 4:1–4].

GOD'S EDUCATION FOR JUSTICE

God's constancy and fidelity as an educator, manifested all through the Old Testament, and central to Jesus' message, appears once more when we speak of the early church as educator. The letter to the Hebrews frequently takes up the subject of correction. Just as God did in the Old Testament, God is still correcting the people. The author of the letter cites a passage from Proverbs in which God is said to "discipline whom he loves" and "scourge every son he receives," and then goes on:

> Endure your trials as the discipline of God, who deals with you as sons. For what son is there whom his father does not discipline? If you do not know the discipline of sons, you are not sons but bastards. If we respected our earthly fathers who corrected us, should we not all the more submit to the Father of spirits, and live? [Heb. 12:7-9].

The author is insisting on the salvific nature of that education, in the form of correction whose finality is the attainment of life, and whose fruit is peace and justice, as appears in verse 11 of the same passage.

Other passages specify the means that God utilizes in divine education in and for justice, namely, Scripture and grace.

> All Scripture is inspired by God and is useful for teaching— for reproof, correction, and training in holiness . . . [2 Tim. 3:16].

The grace of God has appeared, offering salvation to all men. It trains to reject godless ways and worldly desires, and live temperately, justly, and devoutly in this age . . . (Tit. 2:11-12).

SOME CONCLUSIONS

The numerous biblical passages we have cited in Part 2 afford us but an inkling of the extent of the work of interpretation and hermeneutics to be done from the perspective of the Latin American reality. God the educator, revealed all through the Bible, has not ended the work of education with the last page of the Bible. But in order to discern God's educating presence in Latin America today, it will be important to be able to interpret and apply some of the guidelines we have discovered throughout the Old and New Testaments. By way of concluding the second part of this book, let us suggest certain routes along which this work of interpretation and application might proceed.

First, there is no single model of education in the Bible that we could apply deductively to the Latin American reality. Religious education in the Bible is never separated from education for life.

Second, education in the Bible is profoundly bound up with the destiny of the people of God, and this destiny provides education with its objectives, content, and methodology.

Third, education in the Bible is of a piece with the advances and retreats experienced by the people of God throughout the whole history of salvation, and hence enjoys no linear, progressive development. In this sense it is profoundly dialectical.

Fourth, education in the Bible is always linked to the utopia experienced by the people in their longings and aspirations, in its various historical expressions—the land of promise, the covenant, messianism, the kingdom of God, and so on. This utopia is deeply identified with the liberative events that lie at its foundation: the exodus, creation, the covenant of Shechem, Jesus' praxis, the cross and resurrection, the gift of the Holy Spirit, and so on.

Fifth, education in the Bible is popular. God educates through the people. There is an ongoing effort to reconstruct and update the popular memory. The present is always read in the light of the liberative facts and deeds of the past that have constituted the people and their calling to freedom.

Finally, we think that it will be important and helpful to call attention to a process, visible even in the Bible, which will profoundly mark the development of Christian education all through the history of the churches to the present day: there is an evolution in education, both in the Old Testament and the New, in the form of a tendency to institutionalize all the forms and content of education.

In the Old Testament, education began with the immediate application of a reading of history to the transformation of the current state of affairs. Then, over the course of the centuries, education gradually stagnated in the complicated, fleshless teachings of the doctors of the law in the synagogues. In the New Testament the life and practice of Jesus, with all its educational thrust and motivation, tended to be transformed into a doctrine that gradually escaped the monopoly of the believing people.

In a word, there is a tendency to abandon the dynamics that move from the liberative event to a faith reflection on that event and the transformation of the present in the light of the past.

Teaching is systematized. It becomes doctrine and, in the worst case, ideology.

We see this same process in Latin America. In order to discern it and overcome it, it will be indispensable for us today to have a clear perception of the forms of Christian education in Latin America. Without that perception, we shall not be able to restore Christian education to its liberative, popular dynamism and thrust. This will be the subject of the third part of this book.

PART 3

THE MARKS OF A LIBERATIVE CHRISTIAN EDUCATION

We begin this third part with a fact that we have already cited, and which we interpret in a decidedly partisan way: when the poor become the agents of Christian education, Christian education becomes liberative and popular.

The option in which our interpretation consists emerges from a practice of accompaniment of the people in their struggles for liberation—ultimately, in their faith practice. This option emerges from a particular reading of reality—a particular reading of the three models of Christian education that we examined in Part 1—combined with a reading of the Bible in Part 2 that has seen God engaged in the work of education, all through history, through the people.

Now we shall attempt to identify the main characteristics of a liberative Christian education for Latin America, in milieus both conditioning that education and feeling its repercussions. Taking our leave of historical or current problems posed by a "Christian education," spiritualistic or liberal, let us turn our whole attention to an analysis of the possibilities and difficulties attaching to the project of a liberative Christian education. Let us pose some of the major questions that arise in succeeding chapters.

1. What is the relationship of a liberative Christian education to the social structure in general and to the project for society for which the oppressed are struggling? What place does a liberative Christian education occupy here? (chap. 8).

2. If a liberative Christian education is one of the manifestations of the irruption of the poor in the church, what relationship will it have with the church, and specifically, with the church of the poor? (chap. 9).

3. What relationship will this education have to that faith reflection known as theology, which develops from the practice of liberation, in the light of faith? (chap. 10).

4. Finally, inasmuch as we are dealing with a specifically pedagogical process, what will be the interrelationships of a liberative Christian education with the pedagogy of the popular masses emerging in Latin America? (chap. 11).

We propose to conclude Part 3 with a definition of a liberative Christian education. In the meantime, let us understand "Christian education" in the sense of a liberative, popular Christian education.

8

Christian Education and Society:
Conflictual Marks of Christian Education

Christian education, while it has particular traits, is, after all, education, and thus shares the mediations of education in general in the latter's relationship to society. It also shares the opportunities and limitations of education in general, which vary from one social formation to another or, rather, which vary in proportion to the varied success of the advance of the popular movement in its struggle for an alternative society.

Idealistic slogans, so thoroughly interiorized by the ordinary person and by the people, such as "To transform society you must first educate its citizens," and "To have responsible, conscientious Christians, the first step is to give them a Christian education," must be energetically refuted, and this will require a clear notion of the margin for action enjoyed by Christian education, hence by education, within the dependent, backward Latin American societies.

In this chapter we shall attempt to determine which "instances" constitute the channels of the relationship of education with the global social structure, and what the nature of the relationship is between Christian education and ideology, Christian education and economics, and Christian education and politics. We shall ask ourselves what type of autonomy education enjoys vis-à-vis these conditioning elements.

Our point of departure will not consist solely in the "room" left for education by the dominant system, such as a functionalist approach would involve—leaving intact the foundations upon which the present unjust, inegalitarian society rests. We shall look for the cracks in the walls of the dominant system that have been caused by the popular movement. We shall try to see what ground that movement is gaining through its specific struggles, and how the accumulated economic and political victories are, after all, the best education, and the very content of popular education. We shall see how, as the people organize for their own historical project, they not only educate themselves but become *the* genuine educator.

EDUCATION AND THE BASIC INSTANCES OF SOCIAL STRUCTURE

Let us begin with the fact that social structure is shaped by three basic instances: the economic, the political, and the ideological. Let us quickly identify the place occupied by education in this social structure, which is ultimately determined by the economic element. Frequently the attempt has been made to limit the relationship between education and society to the relationship between education and ideology or culture. Taking a more serious view of things, we see that education is profoundly linked to all three basic instances of social structure.

Education and Economics

José C. Mariátegui has written in *Temas de educación* ("The Subject Matter of Education"):

The problem of instruction can be properly understood only if it is considered as an economic problem and a social problem. The mistake of many reformers has been that their method is abstractly idealistic and their doctrine exclusively pedagogical. Their projects have ignored the intimate meshing between economics and instruction, and have sought to modify the latter without knowing the laws of the former. Hence they have succeeded in reforming anything only to the extent of the limits of the consent of economic and social laws [Mariátegui 1970, p. 32].

Education does not occur apart from the functioning of society. It is not an independent instance. It frequently exercises its instance directly through work. Here it must adapt to the requirements of those forms of work that depend on the mode of production, that is, on the economic instance. The capitalist mode of production is based on a technological and social division of work, and education consequently is profoundly marked by the separation obtaining between manual work and intellectual work.

Schematically, we might say that, generally speaking, our education educates the children of employers to be employers and the children of workers to be workers. (It does not educate the children of the unemployed; hence they may continue to be unemployed!)

Education and Politics

We have become too accustomed to draw a hard and fast line between education and politics. Beneath this separation lurks precisely a political project. It would not like to be discovered. We must take the political factor into account if we hope to understand the development of education in Latin America, especially the development of the school. The latter cannot be understood merely as a product of the needs of the productive apparatus—the economic instance. We must also take into consideration the interests and needs of the social groups that are at odds within society. The school is always closely connected to the state. The state at times, in order to maintain its hegemony, needs to broaden its social bases and acquire new support, and so it has recourse to education.

Education and Ideology

We shall define ideology, within a capitalistic society, as that set of ideas, values, and customs that permit the system to reproduce itself, and that bring it about that men and women accept or ignore injustices and basic inequalities, these being principally economic and social.

Ideals generally accepted in society are those of the dominant class. Those who own the means of production, who possess material power, possess spiritual power as well. This is how the oppressive class dominates; this is its only hope of maintaining itself. Falsifying reality, this mechanism represents as the interest of the whole community that which in reality constitutes the interests of a privileged minority.

Within the ambit of ideology, education in general and the school in particular fulfill a basic role, generally through the same functions as employed by ideology, which are mainly three: (1) the function of acceptance and justification: unjust reality is accepted "as is," without any search for the causes of the situation or for a way to change it. "There have always been the poor, and there always will be." (2) the function of distortion: reality is made to appear as the consequence of blind fate, of an irresistible necessity, or of moral shortcomings. "The poor are poor because they're lazy." (3) the function of reproduction: the system reproduces itself by promoting values that benefit itself, suppressing all contrary notions. The dominant class, besides having the capability of coercive violence, also has a power of ideological domination; its "symbolic violence" is much more difficult to discern than the other, but is no less effective.

The Autonomy of Education in Society

We have seen that education is principally mediated through ideology, and that the latter, in turn, depends to a great extent on the economic structure. Now we must ask whether education has any autonomy at all, or whether, instead, it is totally limited by determining factors in society, especially by economics and politics.

There are a number of potential resolutions of this problem, and this, as we shall see, has important implications for Christian education. Three views of the problem are absolute autonomy, absolute determination, and relative autonomy.

Absolute autonomy: Idealism (as a philosophical stance) posits a social change through a change of mentality in individuals considered separately, a change to be effected through education. Education is thus considered to enjoy almost absolute autonomy with respect to economic and political structures.

Absolute determination: At the opposite extreme, a mechanistic materialism posits an absolute determinism of the ideological, and education, by the economic factor. According to this view, education can be no more than a simple reflex of the productive apparatus and the mode of production.

Relative autonomy: Economics, politics, and ideology determine one another reciprocally and mutually, in a dialectical movement. Education is indeed determined, in part, by economic and political factors, but it influences these in its own turn (in varying degrees according to the case). Here, education is not the main factor in social change. The main factor is the transformation of the mode of production and of the distribution of any surplus. But its contribution is crucial. In this third view, various problems or questions that are posed in education receive no narrowly "educational" solution or answer.

CHRISTIAN EDUCATION AND IDEOLOGY

A liberative Christian education, like any other popular educational process, must explain and render explicit its relationships with the dominant ideology. In the case before us, and in the Latin American context, these relationships will have a profoundly critical and conflictual tenor. They will be critical because the dominant ideology in Latin America has, historically, an enormous capacity for the absorption of the religious element in general and Christian symbols and content in particular. They will be conflictual because, ultimately, we are dealing not only with a distinct evaluation and usage of the religious, but with expressions of two radically opposed projects for society: those at the service of a minority, and of the empire, and those at the service of a utopia being constructed by the Latin American people at the price of their struggles and their blood.

We are familiar with the neo-conservative politics of the United States with respect to the religious element, which extends from the most serious and scientific studies of the importance of the religious factor in Latin American societies to the ideological penetration of popular movements via an astounding number of incredibly wealthy sects. In a document entitled *A New Inter-American Policy for the Eighties* (also called the Santa Fe Document), which sketches a United States policy for Latin America for the decade of the 1980s, we find the following statements in the section on education:

The United States must seize the ideological initiative. Encouragement of an educational system in Latin America which emphasizes the common intellectual heritage of the Americas is essential. Education must instill the idealism that will serve as an instrument for survival.

The war is for the minds of mankind. Ideo-politics will prevail. . . .

Thus, while technical training is necessary to material progress, philosophical education is paramount. For the two great questions of every age—"Who am I?" and "What am I doing here?"—remain. . . .

We should . . . export ideas and images which will encourage individual liberty, political responsibility and respect for private property [CSF 1980, pp. 32-33].

In this passage, the conflictuality of which we speak is called war!

Christian Education and the Struggle of the Gods

The expression "struggle of the gods" originated in a work by Pablo Richard and others, *The Idols of Death and the God of Life*, an examination of the biblical theme of the contests of Yahweh the Liberator God with the false gods of oppression, in a perspective of the present system of capitalist oppression generative of the sacralizing idols of oppression and death. In it the authors write:

The oppressive world of today is a world of fetishes and idols, of clerics and theologians. The modern capitalist system is growing more religious and pious by the day. Heightened scientific and technical production has been accompanied by an even greater production of gods, cults, temples, and religious and theological symbols. . . .

The poor no longer fight solely against the oppressing classes and their mechanisms of exploitation; now the poor also fight against fetishes, idols, and all sorts of mystical, spiritual, and theological forces [Richard et al. 1983, pp. 3-4].

A liberative Christian education in this context will be profoundly atheistic and anti-idolatrous. In order to proclaim the God of Jesus Christ, it will have to deny the gods that legitimate oppression, even when these appear in Christian garb. A liberative Christian education collides with all of the "Christian educations" that place themselves in the service of oppression—and that so often are "popular" not in their ends, but only in their addressees, inasmuch as they are directed, like the sects, mainly at the more backward sectors of society for the purpose of reinforcing their alienation, justifying their passivity with religious considerations, suggesting avenues of individual escape, or condemning this world in order to escape all social and political responsibility.

Furthermore, these gods of death have a supernatural ability to evacuate all liberative concepts of their content, and to commandeer, misappropriate any expression or symbol that could represent some danger to the "established order."

Christian Education and Utopia

Confronted with the ideological obstacle, as a set of values that justify disorder, inequality, and planned economically and politically consolidated retardation, the popular classes struggle against this system of death. As they make some advances and win some victories in this construction of their own historical project, they begin to create a new awareness within themselves. They call it their "utopia." The people's utopia is the set of values that supports their new project for society, arising as it does not from a mere description of existing reality or some idealistic dream, but from an actual existing practice, which stands in need of depth, breadth, and generalization.

For Gustavo Gutiérrez, utopia has three principal aspects, beginning with its relation to reality. Utopia necessarily implies the denunciation of existing reality because it is the negation of the circumstances occasioning that reality. This denunciation involves a project for the future, a proclamation. Utopia is verified in praxis: "According to Freire, between the denunciation and the annunciation is the time for building, the historical *praxis*. Moreover, denunciation and annunciation can be achieved only *in* the praxis" (Gutiérrez 1973, p. 234). Finally, utopia has links with science. It is the nerve of its creativity dynamism.

Gutiérrez distinguishes between ideology and utopia in the following terms:

> Ideology . . . spontaneously fulfills a function of preservation of the established order. Therefore, also, ideology tends to dogmatize all that has not succeeded in separating itself from it or has fallen under its influence. Political action, science, and faith do not escape this danger. Utopia, however, leads to an authentic and scientific knowledge of reality and to a praxis which transforms what exists. Utopia is different from science but does not thereby stop being its dynamic, internal element.
>
> Because of its relationship to reality, its implications for praxis, and its rational character, utopia is a factor of historical dynamism and radical transformation. Utopia, indeed, is on the level of the cultural revolution which attempts to forge a new kind of man. Freire is right when he says that in today's world only the oppressed person, only the oppressed class, only the oppressed peoples can denounce and announce. Only they are capable of working out revolutionary utopias and not conservative or reformist ideologies. The oppressive system's only future is to maintain its present of affluence [Gutiérrez 1973, p. 235].

A liberative Christian education falls within the framework of utopia—all the more so when the people who create it are a people who reappropriate the symbols and values of the Christian message, as so many popular Latin American sectors are doing at the present moment.

Christian education, then, will assume the aspects of utopia mentioned above. It will (1) maintain a critical relationship to present historical reality, denouncing, especially, the use made by ideology of the religious element—denouncing the idols of death—and proclaiming, within this reality, the God of life; (2) have its verification in a praxis of the transformation of that reality, as it accompanies the people in their struggles and assumes these struggles as part of the educational endeavor itself; and (3) have a rational and scientific side, in a constant reformulation of the knowledge that it strives to impart through the practice of the struggle being waged by the people.

CHRISTIAN EDUCATION AND ECONOMICS

It is no matter of easy evidence to discover direct relationships between Christian education and economics. We have already seen that such relationships are generally mediated by the ideological element. The consequences of a determinate economic system are justified ideologically, with or without the use of Christian expressions.

Nevertheless, Christian education, even in its more lucid manifestations, does not always discern certain more essential characteristics of the prevailing economic system, and tends naïvely to reproduce them.

Christian Education and the Division of Labor

The capitalist economic system rests on a basic principle: the division of labor into manual and intellectual labor, with a clear subordination of the former to the latter.

Certain alternative currents in education have underscored the importance of work, especially of productive work. Certain very interesting experiments have been conducted in an integration of production and training, demonstrating that when human beings transform matter into products, within socialized relations of production, they are educating themselves and transforming themselves as agents.

Christian education has made no incursions into this area. It has limited itself to nonmanual activities, or at least nonproductive ones, thus reproducing the conventional division of labor and holding aloof from the world of production.

CHRISTIAN EDUCATION AND POLITICS

Christian education suffers great conditioning pressures at the hands of politics in Latin America. Dictatorships and National Security regimes seek to delimit the space in which education generally and Christian education in particular will develop. Christian education materials with anything critical to say about dictatorships or militarism are proscribed.

In a conflictual and effervescent political context such as exists in Latin America, Christian education at once acquires a marked political dimension and collides with interests adverse to those of the people. One of the tasks of Christian education consists precisely in a reevaluation of its political dimension, so often caricatured by reactionary spiritualistic currents. For these groups, to say that a Christian education is politicized is the worst of calumnies. A Christian education with the courage to call itself political has the merit of having broken out of the circle of individualism in which history has held it, and of making inroads into the area of the organization of society—with its own specificity and its own tools, borne up by the advances of the popular movement in its struggle for an alternative quality of human intercourse.

Further to all of this: a liberative Christian education, on the internal level, must use adequate means to avoid the reproduction of the political conditions from which it has suffered for centuries. Let us examine two cases.

Christian Education and the Exercise of Power

> The educational project of centers and educational programs directed by Catholics ought to be oriented to the promotion of justice, and to the elimination, in institutions, of any anti-Christian power structure [CIEC 1980, par. 2].

In an educational process, the relationship between educators and those to be educated is a great deal more than an organizational or pedagogical problem. It is a frankly political problem, touching ultimately on the question of the exercise of power. This means that education is linked not only to a technological division of labor—to a distribution of the tasks of a joint undertaking in function of people's abilities and interests—but to a social division of labor as well. Christian education creates a separation between the direct producers of goods (laborers and *campesinos*) and the producers and transmitters of knowledge (clergy, Christian educators, and so on).

A liberative Christian education cannot allow itself to go on reproducing this division. It can no longer be a simple transmission of concepts. It must seek a direct relationship with the world of work. It must seek to discern, within the production process, for example, those formative aspects that can be illuminated from a Christian perspective.

The school—confessional or not—likewise rests on this division of labor. In this context, Christian education will contribute not so much a new content but an alternative evaluation of work:

> In order to correct the excessively academic education in current curricula, as well as the "upward mobility" mentality of our students . . . we must prepare our students in various occupations that will complete their training, ready them for productive work, and guide them to a reevaluation of labor and of the person of laborers, along with rights of these latter [CIEC 1980, par. 14].

> In an education for justice, the importance of labor obliges those responsible for Catholic education to allot more personnel, time, and resources to technical educational institutions.
> We recommend that these establishments foster the creation of forms of communitarian production among their students and alumni, as a means of rising above the exploitation to which they have often been exposed [CIEC 1980, pars. 41–42].

Still, it seems to us, the basic challenge consists not so much in the generation of new "forms" of education as in the recognition that, in unsuspected places, an educational enterprise is already under way that can be Christian, provided Christian education is able to adapt to the framework of a popular, liberative project. The economic struggle is crucial educational terrain. The struggle for the transformation of the relations of production is more crucial still.

A liberative Christian education does not seek a democratization of the relationships between educator and educand simply through their mutual participation in the planning of the educational endeavor. In a liberative Christian education, educators give up once and for all any privileged role they have—all power, in the coercive sense of the word—to take up full identification with the problem of the quality of life of the people, making their contribution from their own training and abilities.

Indeed, as we shall see, the people, once organized, become a collective educator, as, in their struggle for a new society, with their partial victories, they blaze a trail that can be followed by the popular classes and the oppressed. In other words, the educational function is no longer identified with a determinate social status. Now its power is of a new, popular, shared kind.

Christian Education and the Value of Conflict

In traditional Christian education—spiritualistic or liberal—conflict has a markedly negative connotation. To be educated is to avoid conflict. How much more so if the education is Christian! This is based on a completely distorted concept of what the Bible calls "reconciliation," which leaves out of account the element of conflict inherent in the recognition of errors or in pardon. As we have repeatedly pointed out, conflict, especially the social struggle, has an enormous educational value. We have much testimony to the effect that the people do not learn theoretically, at desks in a school, but in the heat of contest, in the concrete struggles where victory and defeat, critically analyzed, allow them either to advance or to regroup in their passage to liberation.

Our inquiry into education in the Old Testament fully corroborates these statements, and reveals their thrust and potential for the renewal of Christian education today.

"I sincerely think that, in this situation of ours, where we realize that people are gradually being dehumanized, we have to prepare ourselves to learn—but to learn the why of things, their true causes, and this isn't something you learn in school. This is something you learn in the daily struggle. We learn it by our experience, as we try to be concerned for others." These are the words of a woman from a poor neighborhood ["Lo que no enseña . . . ," *Páginas*, p. 25].

9

Christian Education and the Church

In chapter 8 we underscored, albeit perhaps too hastily, some of the relationships necessarily obtaining between Christian education and society as a whole. In the context of Latin American society, what clearly emerges by way of conclusion is that the agent of this education is the Latin American people struggling for their liberation. Characteristic of this people is that, together with being an exploited people, they are a believing people, whose faith is sometimes the vehicle for alienating values (the other side of the coin of the ideology of domination), but sometimes as well of an unshakable thrust of resistance and hope. The irruption of the poor within the church has obliged the latter to undertake a fresh consideration of the most important questions of its identity and mission. This historical, and historic, event revolutionizes the relationships between church and Christian education. The latter is no longer subordinated to the church program, but suddenly finds itself in the service of the proclamation and emergence of the kingdom, which is good news for the poor and oppressed.

We shall see that this educational process, immersed as it is in the popular movement, has its own dynamic resources, such as, for example, the base church communities.

IRRUPTION OF THE POOR WITHIN THE CHURCH

The expression "irruption of the poor within the church" denotes the ever more insistent upsurge of the oppressed classes and

103

races in the Latin American historical process and in the Christian community that appears in this process. It implies not that the poor have been absent from this process, but that their cries have finally emerged from suffocation by the ideologies, religious and other, of the oppressor classes.

> The irruption of the poor also is occurring within the established church, producing a religious and ecclesial transformation. The church is experiencing the judgment of God, which breaks into the liberating history of the poor and exploited. It is a moment of ecclesial grace and conversion, an inexhaustible source of a new and demanding spiritual experience. In the people's struggle, the church continues to rediscover its own identity and mission [EATWOT 1981, par. 20].

The celebrated "option for the poor" is a rereading of the biblical message in response to this irruption taking place at the heart of the church, from a point of departure in the situation of death and oppression in which Latin America lives.

REDEFINITION OF THE CHURCH'S MISSION

The event that we have briefly mentioned just above is conflict-reproducing in the highest degree. It sets in relief the antagonistic interests at play in the churches. This calls for a reconsideration of the raison d'être of the church. The result is a new ecclesiology, which has the following characteristics, among others: (1) The church is not the kingdom. Jesus proclaimed and inaugurated the kingdom, not the church. (2) The kingdom is crisis, conflict. It does not come in the form of a potentiality of present existence or reality, but only in a breach, a rupture with present reality. This holds for the church, as well. (3) The church must continue and prolong the reality of the historical Jesus, which is a reality standing in a relation of action with the kingdom; Jesus intended to build the kingdom within a concrete history.

Consequently, the church neither can nor ought merely to preach or to teach. To proclaim or to teach Christ is to do what Jesus did: it is to follow his historical practice, accepting and assuming the conflict that leads to the cross.

. . . If the Church's mission is understood as a doing, an action taken on so that Jesus may be proclaimed as the Christ, then serious conflicts arise, as the Latin American situation proves. The doing in question will be that of Jesus, a doing that will explain Jesus, but in the final analysis it will be a building of the kingdom of God and not a mere giving of information about what the kingdom is or what form it should take. Thus understood, the mission of the Church . . . is . . . a source of conflict because it means defending not the cause of the Church, but an outside cause, that of the poor [Sobrino 1984, p. 207].

THE POOR AS EVANGELIZERS AND EDUCATORS

The church's mission to proclaim and build the kingdom of God is called evangelization—even if historically this term does not suggest a global praxis of the proclamation of the word and of the transformation of global reality. The poor are not simply the preferential addressees of this process. They become the very agents of evangelization as they bring their struggle into relationship to the message and practice of Jesus. Then they evangelize the church, leading it to a rediscovery of the profoundly subversive tenor of the gospel.

Christian education is an integral part of evangelization. For it, too, "a mere giving of information about what the kingdom is or what form it should take" is not enough. It must contribute to "a building of the kingdom of God." No longer are the poor merely the addressees of Christian education. They have become its agents, and the consequences of this "evangelical inversion" are enormous at the level of the definition, planning, and execution of Christian education. They undermine its very foundations.

The church, the theologians, the magisterium no longer hold a monopoly in Christian education. They are no longer the only authorized agents of the definition of its objectives, content, methods, and situations and places of implementation. If they wish to be faithful to the gospel, they must hear the cry of the people, and of their organizations that are engaged in the building of a new society.

A liberative Christian education will not be primarily devoted to repeating what the church says or to bending all its energies to the transmission of the norm of the church's functioning. It will be a tool in the hands of the poor, to be used in the construction of the kingdom of life in its fullness.

Reciprocally, as we read in the final document of the 1982 Assembly of Theologians of the Southern Cone, which was held in Caixas do Sul, Brazil:

> [The church that the Lord invites us to live and proclaim is] a church built by the poor themselves, from a point of departure in their needs and their own way of doing things and expressing themselves. It is a church where the people can speak out their longings, can celebrate the God of life, and, in contact with God's word, engage in the process of liberating their own faith from the prejudices and fears that oppress it. It is a church that will be a space for freedom, for a gladsome, generous communion of sisters and brothers, a place for responsible sharing. It will be a *school of builders of history,* inspiring Christians to become involved in popular organizations, and constantly accompanying those so committed with the light of faith and the power of the love of Jesus Christ [Teólogos del Cono Sur 1982, par. 20].

CHRISTIAN EDUCATION AND THE BASE CHURCH COMMUNITIES

The example we use at the beginning of this book is not a random one. The base church community is the privileged, all but exclusive locus of a liberative Christian education. The base church communities, as the cutting edge of a "new way of being church" amid the conflicts of Latin America, are also an intrinsically suitable ambient for Christian education.

The base communities have become genuine schools of the people. This they are, to be sure, not in the sense of the traditional school, which executes the task of continuing and nurturing social differences, but in the sense of a school of life and change, inserted into the heart of the popular movement.

> The basic ecclesial communities, or popular Christian communities, form an integral part of the people's march, but do

not constitute a movement or political power parallel to the popular organizations, nor do they seek to legitimate them. The Christian communities—through consciousness-raising, popular education, and the development of ethical and cultural values—exercise among the poor a liberating ministry that is an integral part of their specific mission of evangelization, prophecy, pastoral care, and ministering the sacraments [EATWOT 1981, par. 22].

This people of believers, this collective agent of Christian education finds, in the base communities, part of the space that they need for freedom, struggle, and self-education in a single, integral commitment.

CHRISTIAN EDUCATION AND CELEBRATION

We hear a great deal about the people's sense of festival. Of course, this capacity of theirs for celebration, rejoicing, and entertainment is generally misappropriated and distorted by the dominant ideology, which utilizes it either for frankly commercial ends or, worse, for distracting the people from their harsh, concrete struggles. The fiesta becomes a drug, a refuge from the world and its conflicts. Religious festivals, so important in the life of the people, fare no better.

But the irruption of the poor within the church is, in more than one instance, occasioning an important change in this situation. A new spirituality is appearing. A believing people are repossessing their fiestas, and stamping upon them their global experience of struggle. They are reappropriating their symbols, and rediscovering the protest value that these had had and that was snatched from them by the dominant classes. The feast becomes a cry.

Not only are the people rediscovering their ancient religious feasts, and gradually purifying them of the accretion of alienating elements; they are inventing new celebrations as well, celebrations that spring to life from life itself and its conflicts. The occupation of a piece of land, the struggle for water or electricity, winning a lawsuit for the union, a successful strike, worker ownership of a factory—all of these partial victories overflow in celebration.

This new type of celebration has an enormous educational value.

It shows the people their own strength, reinforces their faith, consolidates relationships among them as a unitary group, consolidates organization. In a word, it provides the people with a genuine spirituality for their struggle, a spirituality that, in certain concrete Latin American situations—such as in Central America—comes to be a truly thundrous addition to the process of social change.

Mass or Sunday worship, despite all efforts on the part of pastors and theologians, had lost all of its educational power. Now it is recovering it, through a rediscovery of the best of primitive Christian tradition, in an act of worship that guarantees and proclaims the social equality of a gladsome, if often clandestine, festive cultus.

10

Christian Education and Theology

Traditionally, the relation between Christian education and theology was simple and stunted. Christian education had the mere function of transmitting truths, in a one-way line of communication from the trustees of the truth to those in need of instruction in the same. Christian education was considered a part of pastoral theology, and had no direct role in the determination of the Christian message. Its role was merely instrumental. It had the task of discovering the most suitable techniques for the handing on of truths and for the reproduction of the conditions required for the division of that intellectual labor: on the one hand, basic theological reflection—biblical, dogmatic, and so on—and on the other, Christian education as the bridge for the sole route of communication of the truth.

To speak of a relationship between Christian education and theology in the context of interest to us evidently requires consideration of another type of theology—a theology framed within the social conflict of Latin America, a theology that reflects on faith from within the praxis of the exploited, believing peoples.

A liberative Christian education cannot be simply a tool in the hands of theology, for the latter is no longer practiced in an ivory tower divorced from the world. Theology now seeks to occupy its specific place within the global process of transformation. In this process, theology strikes a relationship with all of the human and social sciences engaged in contributing to the building of a new society, and thus finds itself in a relationship with an interdisciplinary movement of the sciences of education.

EMERGENCE OF THE THEOLOGY OF LIBERATION

This is not the place to rehearse the familiar story of the origins of liberation theology. For our purposes, we need only insist on one very simple fact, but one that is of great importance for education: the theology of liberation has not sprung up in an academic milieu, the sole result of a great deal of poring over dusty tomes by geniuses of renewal. It has sprung up as a reflection—a serious, scientific reflection—on a new phenomenon: the irruption of the popular movement in Latin America and the ever more significant involvement of Christians in that movement. This occurrence, analyzed in light of the gospel message and the social sciences, constitutes a new terrain for the understanding, in our own day, of the revelation of God in Jesus Christ—in other words, for doing theology. This reflection on praxis in the light of faith cannot afford to remain a mere interplay of ideas, when the life and death of the oppressed of Latin America hang in the balance. A theology that proclaims a God of life can develop only within the struggle for life.

Liberation theology would not exist were it not for the awakening of so many persons who seek to actualize their Christian discipleship in the sociopolitical arena. Nor indeed would there be any point in this reflection were it incapable of accompanying a people-on-the-move, pointing the way, ever from within the process itself, toward this people's own hopes, and warning of possible limitations and deviations.

The theology of liberation as "second act" vis-à-vis a transforming, liberative praxis displays a frankly educational dimension. It rescues the intuitions and values of this believing people and systematizes them, focusing them on their historical project as a people on the way to the kingdom. It hands this people a critical mirror, so that this journey of theirs can acquire deep value from the perspective of faith.

HUMAN AND SOCIAL SCIENCES AND THEOLOGY

A relationship to the human and social sciences is constitutive of the theology of liberation. The critical analysis and interpretation of reality is not a consequence or an auxiliary instrument of theological reflection as a help to more efficient pastoral or educational work. It is part of theological reflection itself. God's liberation project for men and women is played out in this world, in history, within the social conflicts that permeate human reality. The analysis of that reality, then, is not a problem of secondary importance.

The revelation presented in the word of God is insufficient to enable us to tear off reality's mask and delve into its entrails, which the dominant ideology is concerned to conceal and distort with such force and aggressiveness. The social sciences enter into all the moments of theological reflection—even into biblical hermeneutics, where it helps us to understand the world of the Bible and our own, since the word of God is found not only in the texts of the past, but in the events of yesterday and today that give life to those texts.

Everything that we have said about Latin American social reality—educational reality and the faith praxis at its heart—must be read and interpreted with a new scientific rationality, which is furnished not by theology, but by the critical social sciences; and not by just any social science, but by the one that, from the view of the oppressed, gives us the tools to transform society.

The relationship between theology and the social sciences, furthermore, will not obtain solely in the area of the analysis of reality and in the area of hermeneutics. This relationship will be global. At every step theology must ask itself whether it has been infiltrated by the dominant ideology, and this question, which must be posed basically in praxis, likewise calls for the contribution of the social sciences.

We need a better understanding of the concrete mechanisms by which ideology constantly enters the edifice of our faith. And we need this understanding not in view of theoretical considerations, but in order to acquire an operational grasp of what the "return trip" will be, the route of de-ideologization. Theological reflection, then, enters into an interdisciplinary relationship with the critical social sciences, while cautiously preserving its own autonomy.

CHRISTIAN EDUCATION AND LIBERATION THEOLOGY

Here we should like to make a more precise analysis of the meaning of the interdisciplinary relations between theology and education, and thus come to see a way to get beyond the relationship of dependency and subordination that has traditionally obtained between theology and Christian education. The following passage from Raúl Vidales will be a help to us in this endeavor.

> In the methodological process itself, liberation theology contains the elements that assure that, coming as it does from praxis, such theology will intrinsically contain a tendency to return to the people themselves as a production belonging to them.
>
> This can be achieved only through a long, patient pedagogical exercise—an exercise that will not, of course, be conceived as a scholarly task of transmission and apprenticeship, but as a labor of authentic production in the area of pastoral theology, performed within, and in the service of, the liberation process.
>
> The faith that enters by pedagogical works and categories not only restores to the people their own existence, transformed, but converts that existence into a tool in the hands of the people, which is not only "productive," but also "transformative" of present living conditions. Here we have a pedagogical task that embraces the globalism and complexity of the people's cultural reality, and, accordingly, involves a "mass" perspective. This is a pedagogical task embracing all levels of the popular struggle, but one that falls most directly onto the terrain of the ideological struggle. The challenges issuing from this task are a constant dare to creativity and specialization [Vidales 1978, pp. 54–55].

Vidales affords us a clear picture of the dialectical nature of the relationship between a liberative Christian education and the theology of liberation. Here theology is educational, and education is theological.

A Theology That Educates

Liberation theology emerges from a practice of transformation, and is directed toward a further practice of transformation assumed by the people. Theology draws its educative nature from this integration of faith reflection and practice. It is no longer a matter of transmitting a deposit of truths—orthodoxy—in such a way as to render them signifying and comprehensible. It is a matter of discovering and rendering explicit, within a historical practice (however ambiguous and limited), the presence of the God of life as manifest in the struggle for justice, in order that the agent of the said practice—the people—may live this presence in a further practice.

In reflecting upon their faith, the Latin American people do theology; and in doing theology they educate themselves.

> Latin American theology has attempted to overcome the most radical dualism in theology: that of the believing subject and history, of theory and practice—not, however, in the sphere of thought but in the real world. It has aimed to recover the meaning of those profound biblical experiences of what it means to understand theologically: namely, that to understand the truth is to do the truth; that to understand Jesus is to follow Jesus; that to understand sin is to take sin upon oneself; that to understand the world's wretchedness is to liberate the world from its wretchedness; that to understand God is to journey to God along the paths of justice [Sobrino 1984, p. 38].

Theological Education

A liberative Christian education is not to be confused with the mere transmission of faith or Christian content. In order that education be Christian, it is not enough that it speak of God, Jesus Christ, or the church. It must lead to an encounter with Jesus Christ in history and the liberation struggle. What Christian education is concerned with is not knowing but living, not only knowledge but action, not only interpretation but transformation. Christian education is an evangelical praxis—a process of action-reflection-action based on the liberating activity of God.

Christian education, therefore, does theology wherever it enjoys a real insertion into the praxis of a believing people who are genuinely "giving an account of its hope," through a practice of transformation.

CHRISTIAN EDUCATION AND THE BIBLE:
A CASE IN POINT

What is being done with the Bible in a church reborn of the people in Latin America, in the base communities especially, seems to us a revealing case for an understanding of the relationships that we are examining between Christian education and theology.

The Latin American people are rediscovering the Bible and reappropriating it. In it they find their own history or, rather, a critical reflection of their present experience. In this process, they educate themselves, they receive new inspiration for their struggle, and they repossess the word. The interpretation of the word of God is no longer the monopoly of the magisterium or of biblical scholars.

To be sure, this phenomenon is not totally spontaneous. It is in some fashion the fruit of educational activity. Someone puts the Bible into the people's hands; someone gives them guidelines for its use. These pastoral agents, whether or not they are competent in the biblical sciences, have made a great contribution both to biblical theology and popular education.

To sum up: in this context, the Bible is functioning as an important theological tool of popular education. It is illuminating, criticizing, and providing thrust for the people's transforming practice. Reciprocally, the Bible is functioning as the pedagogical tool par excellence in the education of the faith. It is not the transmission of the great church dogmas that awakens the faith of the people, but the setting of a critically analyzed reality in confrontation with the principal theme of the Bible—its message of liberation.

11

Christian Education and Popular Education

A decisive role in the process in which the Latin American people are engaged, the process to which we have been referring throughout this book, is played by a series of educational experiments whose characteristics call for further analysis and systematization. Only with the growing momentum of the popular movement will it be possible to develop the genuine pedagogy that is still missing. The dominant system disposes of developed, sophisticated educational systems based on centuries of economic and cultural domination. There is no ready-made alternative system with which to confront these. Such a system is still in the process of development.

In the present chapter we shall underscore some of the burning problems in popular education, and relate them to a liberative Christian education.

THE STRATEGIC PROBLEM OF POPULAR EDUCATION

Experiments in popular education, and efforts to systematize them, have brought to light various currents and stages during recent years.

Conscientization

One of these currents is "conscientization," or "consciousness-raising." The concept has suffered a great deal of distortion, and in certain instances has even been misappropriated by the dominant ideology, which has partially detached it from the psychosocial method in which it appeared, especially in the works of Paulo Freire. The reason why the concept could be so easily misappropriated is that its relation to popular political action has often been represented in a confused or idealistic manner.

The psychosocial method, in its early development, maintains that in order to counter the people's "naïve" or "magical" mentality it is necessary to initiate a "problematical" educational process, one which will transform that mentality into a "critical awareness." An ingenuous mentality is the expression of a situation of oppression and alienation; acccordingly, the oppressed masses must be made aware of their situation, in order thereupon to be motivated to engage in a transformative activity. In synthesis: one must first create a critical awareness—one must first be "conscientized"—and then engage in an "aware activity." The separation of these two steps led many popular educators to divorce educational practice from organizational and political practice.

The Political Dimension of Education

Practice demonstrated, however, that it was impossible to generate a critical awareness solely by means of dialogue and reflection. Hence certain educational experiments began to merge with the process of mass organization and mobilization for a challenge to the prevailing economic, social, and poiitical inequities. However, the tendency was still to consider education and politics as distinct fields of activity, which had somehow to be joined together. The discovery of the political dimension of education was occasioned mainly by the practice of the people.

Popular Education as the Educational Dimension of Political Activity

It has become clear that the natural place of popular education is the actual dynamics of class struggle, the very dynamism of the activity of the popular movement, and that it is impossible to effect any liberative pedagogical action apart from the liberative political practice taken up by the people. To say that educational activity has no other support or point of departure than the actual activity of the masses is not to deny all specificity, and still less all raison d'être, to a liberative education. The latter abides, and varies in function of global social situations. Of course, education must always be committed to a global strategy of action, from which it will draw its sense, its orientation, and the continuity of its activity. Thus the objectives, the content, and the methodology of popular education will have to be determined and reevaluated moment by moment, in order to keep abreast of the results of a study of the process of overcoming the prevailing structures in which the popular classes must live and move.

Applying the foregoing, in a nonmechanical way, to a liberative Christian education, we discover certain elements that we have mentioned before. Once again we are led to insist on the insertion of this education into the actual journey of the Latin American people toward their liberation. For, once more, the people are the educators. Once they grasp the interconnections of their project and overall liberation strategy, they find themselves building the kingdom of life, which comes by way of the popular historical project.

THE METHODOLOGICAL PROBLEM

A pedagogy that seeks to make its contribution from within the process of social change and the popular movement must have a clear methodology. Such a methodology, to guide the objective of reinforcing the popular conquests and class consciousness, and gradually to transform concrete reality in the course of a process or route, is frequently confused with various work methods that implement methodology—methods adapted to distinct situations. It is even confused with mere techniques that may serve as tools of communication or analysis in the hands of the people, thus enabling them to perform in a creative and dynamic way.

Our methodological conception of popular education is based on a dialectical theory of cognition, seeing that—from our standpoint—the logic of the educational process can be none other than the logic of the process of cognition itself. After all, the educational process, when all is said and done, is a process of the creation and re-creation of knowledge.

The dialectical theory of cognition places social practice front and center. That is, it gives priority to the productive, material activity of social classes and the corresponding forms of cultural activity. It treats cognition as an activity that cannot be dissociated from practice.

To begin with practice, theorize upon it, and return to it again; to begin with the concrete, to carry out a process of abstraction, to return once more to the concrete; to start with action, reflect on it, and go back to action again—here we have the logic of the process of cognition. The logic of the educational process, therefore, can be no different: action-reflection-action, practice-theory-practice [Jara 1981, pp. 28–29].

SOME CHARACTERISTICS OF POPULAR EDUCATION

Up to this point we have been using the expressions "liberative education" and "popular education" indiscriminately and synonymously. The term "liberative education" is denominated from the objective of this education; but this objective must be realized within a perspective of social class, with a clear option for the popular class; therefore a liberative education is a popular education.

Conversely, "popular education" is denominated from the subject or agent of education, the oppressed people, in their struggle to overcome the prevailing system of injustice and death. It is popular only in the measure that it struggles for the people's historical project, that is, in the measure that it is liberative.

Thus although the two terms are synonymous in their denotation, we prefer "popular education" in this chapter, as it seems to us that this term has suffered a lesser degree of misappropriation on the part of the dominant ideology than has "liberative education" *(educación liberadora),* which has been all but emptied of meaning.

With a view to a more detailed consideration of the characteristics of popular education, and a better demonstration of its specificity, let us observe certain general aspects that will have to be considered in any attempt at mapping out such an education.

Defining "Popular Education"

Definitions of "popular education" are to be had in abundance, and we shall not presume to offer a new one. Actually, the concept is not at all easy to define adequately. Popular education is too footloose, too flexible a process, too incapable of institutionalization to be "nailed down" in a definition. We may, however, use this one: "By 'popular education' we understand a process of social practice by means of which the people become aware of their historical role in the building of a new society. It is a global process, possessed of all the aspects of that social process" [CELADEC 1982].

Some Philosophical and Practical Presuppositions

1. Popular education begins with a globalizing outlook. It does not posit a purely educational change, or change in awareness, but operates only by way of insertion into the struggles for social change that are assumed by the masses.

2. Popular education is situated in society, and has its role in the class struggle, the social classes having been produced basically by social relations of production.

3. Popular education rejects any sort of "neutrality." It knows that in our society there is no possibility of an education that would waft above the class struggle, and it is keenly aware of the profound educational value of struggle.

4. Popular education is not circumscribed by any particular education, such as that conducted in a school, a neighborhood, a factory, a church, or the like. But these can facilitate the conduct of a popular education to the extent that their activities maintain a relationship with the strategic struggles of a people for a new, alternative society.

5. Popular education simultaneously integrates three levels: the *personal* (fostering an "unblocking," so that an individual functions no longer merely as an individual but as a person); the *communitarian* (inasmuch as it is really in community that we move and can come to self-realization as persons); and the *popular* (on the level of the broader "community," the only matrix in which we can achieve a liberation on the level of social structure).

Some Objectives of Popular Education

Within the breadth and complexity of the objectives of a popular education, let us select just a few, without any regard for order or hierarchy.

1. Participation in the transformation of the prevailing situation of injustice on the various levels at which the struggle is being waged.

2. A contribution to the materialization of the utopia (or counterideology) that is taking shape in the struggle of the oppressed for their liberation, as other values, another type of knowledge, a new project for the human being and society, begin to make their appearance.

3. The acquisition of a critical capacity for the analysis of actual reality, for exposing the mechanisms employed by the dominant ideology for the legitimation and reproduction of the prevailing system.

4. The rediscovery and recovery of autochthonous values, and the revival of the collective memory of struggles and victories already attained.

5. A transcendence of the authoritarian relationship in all human relations in which the pedagogical relationship has a role: man/woman, teacher/pupil, parent/child, adult/young, priest/laity, and so on.

Methods of Popular Education

1. The method of popular education is dialogical and social. Instruction is not the effect of the self-imposition of one person on another, but of the discovery made by a group in its practice of transforming the world.

2. The method of popular education is nonauthoritarian and democratic in the sense that the will to work as a group and the need for a group come ahead of the will of a person, a program, or norms established by third parties.

3. The method of popular education is structured in function of each given situation and conjuncture, starting with the global methodology of transforming activity, reflection, transforming activity.

4. The method of popular education is frankly critical in the sense that it maintains a constant questioning not only of the prevailing social situation, but also of the development of the group in the face of this situation.

Values and Content of Popular Education

The process of discovering the values and content of a popular education is dynamic and ongoing. It would be foolish, then, to list them as if they had already been discovered. But let us point to a few of those being discovered, solely in order to be able to contrast them with the pseudo-values of an "integrating" education: (1) "class belonging": our membership in the class into which we were born; (2) class position: the location of our class in the socioeconomic structure of the system; (3) class option: taking sides with the interests, needs, and values of the popular classes; (4) confidence in our own abilities; (5) creativity, as opposed to formalism and traditionalism; (6) solidarity, as opposed to competition and the like.

CHRISTIAN EDUCATION AND POPULAR EDUCATION

We came to the conclusion, in the second part of this book, that, in conformity with biblical tradition, authentic Christian education will be education in and for life, and that the subject or agent of this education will be the people, whose life is threatened by a system of death. Then we saw that, for Christian education to be Christian and not idolatrous, it must be liberative, or popular.

Reading the Latin American reality, and interpreting the irruption of the poor in this reality, we have seen throughout the third part of this book that this exploited and believing people, in their struggle for a new, alternative, different society, are educating themselves in Christian fashion, in the measure that they repossess the values and symbols of their faith that have been wrested from them by the dominant ideology.

But is it enough for education to be popular in order to be Christian? Committed Christians sometimes seem to have "guilt feelings" about posing the problem of the specificity of Christian education, as if doing so would mean withdrawing from the popular movement and its struggles. As we have already remarked, within the globalism of the struggle for a new society, a specific task is incumbent upon Christians: to live the faith, which is part of the experience of the people, within the global strategy of the kingdom of God and the people's historical project. To posit a specificity of Christian education within the ambit of popular education in no way implies that Christian education will have some other agent than the people, or any project other than that of liberation.

As the document from the CELADEC Workshop states:

> Concretely, in the life of a poor and oppressed people, the potentialities of a liberative faith are bound up with the revolutionary capacity, and vice versa. Neither can be developed without account being taken of the other. Nevertheless, we must reject any attempt at "reductionism," whether in the form of a disincarnate spiritualism that feeds on a rarefied concept of "religious meaning" or in that of a view of political activity that idealistically ignores the faith-reality of the people.
>
>   In current circumstances in Latin America, Christian education, of its very nature, must be popular education, inasmuch as the popular element delivers the historical expression of the [biblical, Christian] message of liberation. Both Christian and popular education are involved in the common task of liberation, but Christian education leads to an empirical commitment of faith, personal and communitarian, that is lived and celebrated at the very heart of historical mediations: struggle, popular organization, the historical project, utopia, and so on [CELADEC 1982].

This empirical, experiential faith-commitment, which is the fundamental mark of a liberative Christian education, is a great deal more than a content to be transmitted. Christian education is characterized not so much by content (easily misappropriated and historically distorted by the dominant ideology) as by its effect: a people living its faith—making it explicit, reflecting upon it, celebrating it, and teaching it—within a practice of sociopolitical transformation.

Clearly, Christian education will have its own content and will seek the best way to communicate it. But this content will have an effect—and a Christian effect—only to the extent that it is related to a transforming practice within a global strategy.

Christian education is not subordinate to popular education. Rather, it must be an integral part of that education if it is to be faithful to its vocation, if it is committed to the God of life, who hears the cry of the people, today, in Latin America.

Abbreviations

CELADEC   Comisión Evangélica Latinoamericana de Educación
Cristiana (Latin American Evangelical Commission for Christian Education)

CIEC   Confederación Interamericana de Educación Católica (Inter-American Alliance for Catholic Education)

CSF   Committee of Santa Fe for the Council of Inter-American Security

EATWOT   Ecumenical Association of Third World Theologians

Works Cited

CELADEC. 1981. *Consulta latinoamericana de educación popular.* Lima: CELADEC.

————. 1982. *Educación cristiana, educación popular.* Lima: CELADEC.

CIEC. 1980. "Metodología de una educación en y para la justicia" (final document of the 13th Inter-American Congress of the CIEC, held in Santo Domingo, Dominican Republic, January 1980). In *Metodología de una educación en y para la justicia.* Bogotá: CIEC.

CSF. 1980. *A New Inter-American Policy for the Eighties.* Ed. Lewis Tambs. Washington, D.C.: Council for Inter-American Security.

EATWOT. 1981. "Final Document: International Ecumenical Congress of Theology, February 20–March 2, 1980, São Paulo, Brazil." In Sergio Torres and John Eagleson, eds., *The Challenge of Basic Christian Communities.* Maryknoll, N.Y.: Orbis Books.

Echegaray, Hugo. 1984. *The Practice of Jesus.* Trans. Matthew J. O'Connell. Maryknoll, N.Y.: Orbis Books.

Girardi, Giulio. *Educación integradora, educación liberadora.* 2 vols. Bogotá: Dimensión Educativa. (Out of print.)

Gutiérrez, Gustavo. 1973. *A Theology of Liberation: History, Politics and Salvation.* Trans. and ed. Caridad Inda and John Eagleson. Maryknoll, N.Y.: Orbis Books.

Jara, Oscar. 1981. *Educación popular: la dimensión educativa de la acción política.* Panama City and San Jose, Costa Rica: CEAPSA/ALFORJA.

Libânio, J. B. 1980. *Formación de la conciencia crítica.* 3 vols. Bogotá: CLAR.

"Lo que no enseña el colegio se aprende en la lucha diaria." *Páginas* 45 (1982).

Mariátegui, José C. 1970. *Temas de educación.* Lima: Biblioteca Amauta.

Richard, Pablo, et al. 1983. *The Idols of Death and the God of Life: A Theology.* Trans. Barbara E. Campbell and Bonnie Shepard. Maryknoll, N.Y.: Orbis Books.

Sobrino, Jon. 1984. *The True Church and the Poor.* Trans. Matthew J. O'Connell. Maryknoll, N.Y.: Orbis Books.

Teólogos del Cono Sur. 1982. *Documento final de la reunión de los teólogos del Cono Sur* (final document of the assembly of the Theologians of the Southern Cone, held at Caixas do Sul, Brazil, in 1982).

Vidales, Raúl. 1978. "La producción teológica desde la tradición de los pobres." In *Desde la tradición de los pobres.* Teología Latinoamericana, no. 5. Mexico City: CRT.

Other Orbis Titles. . .

PEDAGOGIES FOR THE NON-POOR
by Robert A. Evans, Alice Frazer Evans & William Bean Kennedy
Three years of research and consulation provide data for these eight cases focusing on consciousness-raising education in a North American context. Among the critical commentators on the cases are Suzanne Toton, F. Ross Kinsler, Kosuke Koyama, and Philip Scharper. An interview with Paulo Friere on these pedagogical processes is also included. Discussion questions and suggested readings follow each case.
no. 409-7   302pp. pbk.

EDUCATION FOR PEACE
Testimonies from World Religions
edited by Haim Gordon & Leonard Grob
The thesis of this book is that at their cores the world religions contain resources that are the most viable and practical basis for peace education and for authentic peacemaking. Representatives of Judaism, Christianity, Islam, Buddhism, and Hinduism provide overviews of the theme of peace in their respective scriptures and traditions; other essays focus on the practical aspects of implementing peace education. The book is addressed to students (undergraduate and graduate) and professors in peace studies and comparative religion departments, and those in the peace movement interested in and searching for new and traditional religious and spiritual wellsprings for their actions.
no. 359-7   224pp. pbk.

THE CATHOLIC PEACE TRADITION
by Ronald G. Musto

Not only Protestants but also Catholics have tended to associate pacifism with Protestant peace churches. So when the U. S. Catholic Conference of Bishops issued their peace pastoral in 1983, many Christians were unaware that the pastoral was part of a continuing, unbroken stream of pacifism and peacemaking within Catholicism dating back to the early church. At last, students, teachers, clergy, and laypeople now have in one volume a readable history of the Catholic peace tradition from its biblical antecedents to the twentieth century.

Ronald Musto is especially concerned to show Catholics who oppose war and militarism that their commitment to peacemaking is not a radical departure from the past, but an integral part of their religious tradition. He elaborates the different forms that Catholic peacemaking has taken historically in an attempt to provide today's Catholics with a strong connection to a vital heritage. Musto's focus on the decisive role of people's movements in sustaining the message of peace will empower individuals and groups involved in antiwar activities.

no. 263-9   464pp. pbk.

COMMUNICATION FOR ALL
The Churches and the New World Information and Communication Order
edited by Philip Lee

The media of information and communication has long been dominated by the First World. The result has been a lack of impartial information about the poorer, marginalized countries, particularly those of the Third World, and inadequate analysis, due to cultural bias, of Third World issues. In an effort to combat this problem, a New World Information and Communication Order (NWICO) has been proposed that aims to develop a more democratic, decentralized, participatory communication system. The NWICO proposal is based on the contention that communication is an inseparable part of the social process and that professional communicators must look at their activities in relation to the difficulties of peoples and nations throughout the world.

This book provides a thorough examination of the world's present communication system, the NWICO proposal, and the challenges that NWICO presents to the churches. It will be read with interest by all who are concerned about the negative effects of First World domination on Third World societies as well as by anyone interested in information and communications industries.

no. 246-9   176pp. pbk.

JUSTICE AND PEACE EDUCATION
Models for College and University Faculty
edited by David M. Johnson

A collection of models for integrating justice and peace concerns into courses in various disciplines ranging from the humanities, the social sciences, and interdisciplinary studies to business, management, and engineering. Based on the practical educational and research experience of professors in U.S. Catholic colleges and universities, each model includes a course syllabus, a list of required texts for students, and suggested readings for faculty. The result is an intelligent, pragmatic manual for educators seeking to promote a more just and peaceful world. Contributors include Monika Hellwig, William Byron, David O'Brien, Marie Augusta Neal, Thomas Shannon, and Suzanne Toton.

 no. 247-7   256pp. pbk.